"The Object Lessons series achieves something very close to magic: the books take ordinary—even banal—objects and animate them with a rich history of invention, political struggle, science, and popular mythology. Filled with fascinating details and conveyed in sharp, accessible prose, the books make the everyday world come to life. Be warned: once you've read a few of these, you'll start walking around your house, picking up random objects, and musing aloud: 'I wonder what the story is behind this thing?'"

Steven Johnson, *author of Where Good Ideas Come From and How We Got to Now*

"Object Lessons describe themselves as 'short, beautiful books,' and to that, I'll say, amen. . . . If you read enough Object Lessons books, you'll fill your head with plenty of trivia to amaze and annoy your friends and loved ones—caution recommended on pontificating on the objects surrounding you. More importantly, though . . . they inspire us to take a second look at parts of the everyday that we've taken for granted. These are not so much lessons about the objects themselves, but opportunities for self-reflection and storytelling. They remind us that we are surrounded by a wondrous world, as long as we c   look."

une

Besides being beautiful little hand-sized objects themselves, showcasing exceptional writing, the wonder of these books is that they exist at all. . . . Uniformly excellent, engaging, thought-provoking, and informative."

Jennifer Bort Yacovissi,
Washington Independent Review of Books

. . . edifying and entertaining . . . perfect for slipping in a pocket and pulling out when life is on hold."

Sarah Murdoch, *Toronto Star*

For my money, Object Lessons is the most consistently interesting nonfiction book series in America."

Megan Volpert, *PopMatters*

[W]itty, thought-provoking, and poetic . . . These little books are a page-flipper's dream."

John Timpane, *The Philadelphia Inquirer*

Though short, at roughly 25,000 words apiece, these books are anything but slight."

Marina Benjamin, *New Statesman*

OBJECT LESSONS

A book series about the hidden lives of ordinary things.

Series Editors:

Ian Bogost and Christopher Schaberg

Advisory Board:

Sara Ahmed, Jane Bennett, Jeffrey Jerome Cohen, Johanna
Drucker, Raiford Guins, Graham Harman, renée hoogland,
Pam Houston, Eileen Joy, Douglas Kahn, Daniel Miller,
Esther Milne, Timothy Morton, Kathleen Stewart, Nigel
Thrift, Rob Walker, Michele White.

In association with

LOYOLA UNIVERSITY NEW ORLEANS   Georgia Tech | Center for Media Studies

BOOKS IN THE SERIES

Remote Control by Caetlin Benson-Allott

Golf Ball by Harry Brown

Driver's License by Meredith Castile

Drone by Adam Rothstein

Silence by John Biguenet

Glass by John Garrison

Phone Booth by Ariana Kelly

Refrigerator by Jonathan Rees

Waste by Brian Thill

Hotel by Joanna Walsh

Hood by Alison Kinney

Dust by Michael Marder

Shipping Container by Craig Martin

Cigarette Lighter by Jack Pendarvis

Bookshelf by Lydia Pyne

Password by Martin Paul Eve

Questionnaire by Evan Kindley

Hair by Scott Lowe

Bread by Scott Cutler Shershow

Tree by Matthew Battles

Earth by Jeffrey Jerome Cohen and Linda T. Elkins-Tanton

Traffic by Paul Josephson

Egg by Nicole Walker

Sock by Kim Adrian

Eye Chart by William Germano

Whale Song by Margret Grebowicz

Tumor by Anna Leahy

Jet Lag by Christopher J. Lee

Shopping Mall by Matthew Newton

Personal Stereo by Rebecca Tuhus-Dubrow

Veil by Rafia Zakaria

Burger by Carol J. Adams

Luggage by Susan Harlan

Souvenir by Rolf Potts

Rust by Jean-Michel Rabaté

Doctor by Andrew Bomback

Fake by Kati Stevens

Blanket by Kara Thompson

High Heel by Summer Brennan

Pill by Robert Bennett

Potato by Rebecca Earle

Email by Randy Malamud

Hashtag by Elizabeth Losh

Magnet by Eva Barbarossa

Coffee by Dinah Lenney (forthcoming)

Compact Disc by Robert Barry (forthcoming)

Fog by Stephen Sparks (forthcoming)

Ocean by Steve Mentz (forthcoming)

Pixel by Ian Epstein (forthcoming)

Train by A. N. Devers (forthcoming)

hashtag

ELIZABETH LOSH

BLOOMSBURY ACADEMIC
NEW YORK • LONDON • OXFORD • NEW DELHI • SYDNEY

BLOOMSBURY ACADEMIC
Bloomsbury Publishing Inc
1385 Broadway, New York, NY 10018, USA
50 Bedford Square, London, WC1B 3DP, UK

BLOOMSBURY, BLOOMSBURY ACADEMIC and the Diana logo are trademarks of
Bloomsbury Publishing Plc

First published in the United States of America 2020

Cover design: Alice Marwick

Bloomsbury Publishing Inc does not have any control over, or responsibility for,
any third-party websites referred to or in this book. All internet addresses given in this
book were correct at the time of going to press. The author and publisher regret any
inconvenience caused if addresses have changed or sites have ceased to exist,
but can accept no responsibility for any such changes.

Library of Congress Cataloging-in-Publication Data
Names: Losh, Elizabeth M. (Elizabeth Mathews), author.
Title: Hashtag / Elizabeth Losh.
Description: New York : Bloomsbury Academic, 2019. | Series: Object lessons |
Includes bibliographical references and index.
Identifiers: LCCN 2019010119 (print) | LCCN 2019010759 (ebook) | ISBN
9781501344282 (ePub) | ISBN 9781501344299 (ePDF) | ISBN 9781501344275
(pbk.: alk. paper)
Subjects: LCSH: Hashtags (Metadata) | Social media.
Classification: LCC P302.37 (ebook) | LCC P302.37 .L67 2019 (print) | DDC
302.23/1–dc23
LC record available at https://lccn.loc.gov/2019010119

ISBN: PB: 978-1-5013-4427-5
ePDF: 978-1-5013-4429-9
eBook: 978-1-5013-4428-2

Series: Object Lessons

Typeset by Deanta Global Publishing Services, Chennai, India
Printed and bound in the United States of America

To find out more about our authors and books visit www.bloomsbury.com and
sign up for our newsletters.

This book is dedicated to Felix Horan with many heart emojis.

CONTENTS

#Hashtag 1

#Octothorpe 9

#Inventor 19

#Person 25

#Place 39

#Slogan 61

#Brand 75

#Origin 85

#Intersection 89

#Noise 93

#Chatter 99

#File 113

#Metadata 123

#Acknowledgments 131
Notes 134
Index 142

#HASHTAG

A hashtag toppled a dictator. A hashtag emboldened an authoritarian leader.

A hashtag launched a product. A hashtag eviscerated a corporation

A hashtag commemorated a murdered person. A hashtag threatened to murder a person.

How can such a short string of text claim to accomplish so much noteworthy political, economic, and cultural action? Even without recognizable words, a hashtag can make a profound statement. For example, Turkish feminists used #Kahkaha to imitate the sound of guffawing after the country's deputy prime minister claimed that nice women didn't laugh in public.

Cynics insist that digital activity has little or no impact on the violence and suffering of the real world. Online behavior may even contribute to the misery of the oppressed. In the push and pull of social media, human rights activists use the same platforms as those rooting for genocide, martial law, or capital punishment. Within months leaders of revolutions in the Arab Spring lost ground to strongmen with equally potent hashtags.

Nonetheless, hashtags are an important way for people to talk to other people. And hashtags are a way for machines to talk to other machines.

A hashtag, as Wikipedia explains, is "a type of metadata tag" that groups similarly tagged messages or allows an electronic search to return all messages that contain the same hashtag. It uses a word, abbreviation, acronym, or unspaced phrase prefixed with the hash character (#) to form a label. In other words, the hash symbol tells the computer that a particular word or words should be read as more important than other words in a given message for purposes of sorting digital content into similar clusters.

The #hashtag actually exists in two pieces, with two separate but related design histories. The # is a special kind of character used to facilitate communication involving nonhumans. The "pound sign" or "number sign" existed long before it first appeared on Remington typewriters in the 1800s, and it has been used for almost a century to give special instructions to machines. The letters after the # also are part of a bigger narrative about naming conventions. It is the story of metadata, data about data.

Individual hashtags may seem to be novelties falling in and out of fashion, but the entire life of the hashtag and its ancestors has been long, rich, and contested. The talkative technologies that have used the hash symbol (#) date back centuries and include the ledger, the typewriter, the Teletype, the touch-tone phone, the computer, and the smart phone. The human designers, consumers, searchers, indexers, and censors who organize information with metadata represent an even more diverse population. Their purposes run the gamut from social justice activism to brand promotion to totalitarian message control to the everyday emotional maintenance of the bonds of friendship.

As an object, a hashtag aspires to prominence, but it has a tendency to disappear as a specific artifact assembled from distinct components. The hashtag as an assemblage of individual characters is usually only appreciated for its utility as a handy informational label or a finding aid.

To the weary and confused the hashtag provides a signpost to a specific island otherwise lost in a vast archipelago of possible destinations in a sea of information overload. On a map of trending topics it may sound like a foreign collection of letters, such as #MAGA. Like any isolated island, however, once people clamber ashore, a hashtag marks a place where members either build community or fight over scarce resources.

In theory, to be used effectively by people promoting a cause, project, or product, hashtags should be simultaneously short, unique, memorable, unambiguous, resistant to variant spelling, and descriptive as content labels. Yet many common hashtags fail at least one of these tests. This occurs either because the name was decided upon by just one person with little forethought or because it was forged over a long period of time by a bureaucratic group with diverse interests, like the camel assumed to be a horse designed by a committee.

Inelegant and unpronounceable hashtags like #VZWInnovate survive because loyal maintainers keep them in use. These upright citizens remind others to insert hashtags consistently and correctly. They model ways to use hashtags as part of a common language. The stories of these hashtag caretakers are just as significant as those of the hashtag inventors who first may have brought them into use. The larger tale of the hashtag also includes those who choose to destroy a specific hashtag, often by "hijacking" a once-useful label by turning it into something odious to former users.

Sometimes it might seem that there is no rhyme nor reason to picking a good hashtag, but some common strategies include choosing proper names of people who would not otherwise be famous (#SandraBland, #TrayvonMartin), specific geographical places (#Ferguson, #IndiaGate), slogans (#HandsUpDontShoot, #ThisIsWhatDisabilityLooksLike), brands (#Nike, #Apple), and events (#Coachella, #BurningMan). Although hashtags are very condensed as expressive cultural artifacts, like other pieces of writing they merit the scrupulous attention paid to a poem or short story in unpacking their complexity and decoding all the influences and historical context that may have informed their production.

For many years I have taught writing, have directed writing programs, and have written writing textbooks. Because of my specialization, people often ask me questions about writing in terms of right and wrong behavior. Like most writing specialists working today I adopt a rhetorical approach to teaching writing that de-emphasizes mechanical errors in standard English and instead focuses on the specific situations in which people write, the audiences they are addressing, and the purposes they hope to achieve by undertaking a written composition.

Rules and correctness still matter, but writing conventions are most useful if they allow some flexibility, particularly as a way to encourage beginners. Just as most people learn to be better speakers of a foreign language by practicing with people they respect and care about or by striving to achieve personal goals, most people learn to be better writers by paying more attention to context. That's the principle of rhetorical mindfulness that is central to hashtag use. Adept users must pay attention to how a hashtag conveys the credibility, emotional availability, and rationality that they wish to project. Successful hashtaggers must be aware of the presence of specific audiences, the best way to advance particular purposes, and the details of new situations that arise.

Of course, because hashtags are read by a computer, like all instructions given to a machine, precision matters. Our nonhuman companions have difficulty reading contextually, and computers are often unable to interpret instructions that contain misspellings or errors. Using the wrong hashtag can stymie communication even before rhetoric comes into play.

Like its author, chances are that many readers of this book don't use hashtags in their everyday digital communication. If they do, they might feel silly or exhibitionistic doing it. They might even think people who use hashtags are ridiculous, particularly when they pronounce them in full out loud, like young people bellowing "Hashtag-FOMO" or "Hashtag-YOLO" to their friends. Comedians on late-night television depending on laughs may pepper their jokes with hashtags for humorous effect.

Hashtags can even seem a sign of poor judgment. It might be difficult to imagine why the rapper Dappy of the group N-Dubz got a hashtag tattoo near his right eye "2 make sure" his face "stays trending 4 ever." British tabloids were quick to mock the young man, whose real name, Costadinos Contostavlos, seemed a mouthful of letters, for permanently branding himself.

However, learning to think through the context in which the text of a hashtag is used can be a good way to become a more apt digital communicator, which people of all ages and backgrounds must do. So even if many examples in this book come from faraway places around the world, the difficult problem of what to name something to help a particular message travel or be findable should be applicable to many issues close at home.

The rhetorical approach to thinking about hashtags can also raise questions that don't have easy answers or practical tips. There are philosophical dilemmas and existential quandaries that can't be easily resolved about how to name things, particularly given the large role that nonhuman reading and writing machines now play in our daily lives. These devices might be in incomprehensible communication loops with us, constantly pinging us with messages that we can't see, much less decode, or they might only speak to other machines in long relays to which we don't have access and bypass us as human minders entirely. Because the hashtag is something that is visible to us but also intended for computational communication, it allows us to think about the things that machines might be saying behind our backs.

Machine-to-machine communication has a long history that predates the advent of the digital computer and distributed networks like the Internet. Eighteenth-century tinkerers with basic knowledge of static electricity fiddled with pith balls to get one device to converse with another. Others proposed elaborate contraptions made of tubes threaded with wires for each letter of the alphabet intended to make pieces of gold leaf shiver in response at either end. Later, a century of sophisticated single-wire electric telegraphy energized the modern stock market and enabled the rise of European and American colonial power.

Yet the more recent story of machine-to-machine communication diverged in important ways from the path set by the previous period of mechanical and electrical systems designed for displaying, disseminating, and storing information. Machines that depended upon informational architectures optimized for semiconductors and optical fibers took advantage of increasingly global protocols for conversations between nonhuman agents, protocols that often privileged the English language and Internet addresses in the Global North.

This period of standardization epitomized twentieth-century modernism and the development of ambitious cybernetic communication platforms that optimized how a computer approximated human intelligence. To successfully transmit messages to that non-human intelligence, new user interfaces would be required. A massive experiment in reengineering an apparatus initially designed for transmitting human voices—the telephone—would be critical to its success.

#OCTOTHORPE

When John F. Kennedy entered the digits 1-9-6-4 on the touch-tone telephone in the White House, he helped launch a new age of telecommunication. This newfangled apparatus had been installed in the Oval Office as part of an elaborate publicity stunt for the New York World's Fair. The sequence of four numbers initiated a countdown clock for the fair's opening in 1964, a year the president would not live to see. Although Kennedy had crossed out crassly capitalistic terms like "companies" and "industries" from his speech for the touch-tone ceremony, the Bell System intended to place its corporate branding firmly on the 1964 fair, just as it had on the 1962 fair in Seattle.

A promotional film from the Seattle fair, *Century 21 Calling,* presents the AT&T corporate pavilion as a didactic center where the public could encounter new ideas about machine-to-machine communication for the first time. In the movie, the concept is introduced with an easy-to-understand scenario: dialing machines in different cities that play recordings about the weather. Then telephones are shown giving instructions to ovens, air conditioners, and sprinkler systems, ordering far away objects to turn themselves on or off.

The designers at Bell Labs knew that telephones were not always intuitive devices to use. The nineteenth-century convention of saying the relatively recent word "hello" after picking up a ringing phone was introduced through an extended pedagogical process, which included instructions printed in early telephone books. Alexander Graham Bell felt that "ahoy" was a better opening response, but Thomas Edison prevailed with the greeting still used in English-speaking countries today.

In the AT&T film about the Seattle World's Fair many products and services new to telephones of the 1960s are explained: call forwarding, three-way calling, call waiting, and paging. To understand these new telephonic practices a Bell spokeswoman with a bouffant hairdo introduces her audience to the company's masterful "electronic brain." In a carefully enunciated presentation, the woman describes how this aggregation of "magical" and "amazing" micro-components "will not only carry out instructions you dial into it; it will also remember instructions you provided earlier."

The electronic brain connected to the touch-tone phone is shown an active problem solver in the film, capable of interrupting a female busybody, forwarding a call from a handsome man in a military uniform, and phoning grandma more easily. The spokeswoman describes the process in the simplest terms possible.

Now let's say you want to call your mother who lives in Des Moines. You call her fairly often so the telephone company has assigned 53 as your special number for making this call. When you dial the five and the three the electronic central office's brain says "uh oh something special," searches its memory for what those two digits represent, and dials the area code plus the phone number in Des Moines for you.[1]

According to the woman in the Bell pavilion, the symbolic logic of the two-digit code should elicit an exclamation from the surprised computer when it senses an interruption in its otherwise monotonous routine. Eventually the pound and asterisk symbols would flag coded instructions using the customer's telephone keypad. But the places for those cryptic signs were still blank on the phones in the World's Fair pavilions.

Like the pigeons in the fair's Skinner Box demonstration, the visitors to the touch-tone pavilion were part of a behavioral experiment. Bell Labs was an innovator in user-centered design, and the fair was a place for its corporate parent AT&T to test the feasibility of experimental prototypes on a massive scale. The pushbutton phones that were poked and prodded in the fair's demonstrations had evolved after an arduous period of trial and error. For almost a decade designers had been preparing for this radical transformation, because abandoning the rotary dial required a complete mutation of the face of the instrument. The ingenious pushbutton mechanism that distributed force through the plunger and contact assembly with the aid of two springs—a snap spring and a helical spring—was relatively straightforward. The problem was that the rest of the telephone's anatomy had to be completely reimagined without its vestigial disk.

The central decision about how to arrange the numbers for easy and accurate dialing wasn't completely self-evident. Because many legacy technologies were still in use, developed by competing companies in disparate regions, there were multiple choices and proponents for each spatial arrangement of buttons. A toll operator's keyset consisted of two vertical columns with the "0" and "9" at the base. The numbering order went up the left column and down the right. In contrast adding machine keypads organized the numbers mostly in rows of three, with the numbering running from left to right and bottom to top.

Psychologists attempted to tackle the problem using theories about human expectations. They reasoned that if anticipation matched reality then learning something new—like pushing buttons rather than turning a wheel—could be accomplished much more easily. One 1955 study jettisoned all the existing configurations and invited participants to start from scratch. Subjects were given a booklet with buttons to fill in, unlimited time to complete the task, and erasers if they changed their minds. Fifty-five out of a hundred subjects picked the configuration we have today.[2]

Achieving a bare majority wasn't decisive enough, so experts in industrial efficiency tried a range of physical prototypes. A 1960 article in the *Bell Telephone Journal* includes illustrations of some of the more fanciful choices including a rainbow, a diagonal stair-step, and a pyramid. Engineers brought in custom-built monitoring equipment for assessing dialing performance, including a keyed number indicator, an error indicator, a time clock, and a recording mechanism.[3] According to their findings, the uncrowded configuration in the old circle pattern might produce the greatest accuracy for one experimental group, but two horizontal rows might be significantly faster for another. The shape, size, and spacing of the buttons were all hotly debated, although everyone agreed that the "0" key needed to be isolated on the interface.

Without clear consensus emerging, Bell designers abandoned what must have become a dreary routine of button-pushing and number-crunching. They returned to imagining the phone as a Platonic ideal. Teams from the lab went back to encouraging users to draw their perfect phone pad, and the configuration was finalized. The process involved years of intense human factors engineering, but with only ten variables it was a combinatorial innovation that could never be patented.

The twelve-button touch-tone telephone was introduced in 1968 with the * key and # key designed for new computer services. As in the case of the ten-button version of the phone, many other possibilities had already been rejected. An earlier version used completely different symbols. In successful field trials the keys next to the "0" key had been marked with a five-pointed star and a diamond. One member of the Bell Labs team, Doug Kerr, claimed that the star and diamond signs had to be swapped out to comply with the new ASCII character set for computers.[4] ASCII is a common library of letters, numbers, and symbols still in use today. The phrase "ASCII is forever" is familiar to many programmers who know that computer languages and platforms may come and go but certain basic coding conventions remain.

Kerr thought that using ASCII would ensure exact correspondence in communication between the telephone and the device with which it was conversing. This precision was important because variability in deciding how a symbol should be decoded could introduce uncertainty and garble messages. In the Teletype machine, an earlier pre-ASCII technology, certain combinations of five-bit code could be used for more than one symbol. Such teleprinters or teletypewriters were semi-automated devices used for communicating text over telegraph lines, telephone networks, Telex systems, radio relays, or satellite links. Unlike the narrow lexicon of Morse code, the Teletype alphabet had a larger range of characters and included useful symbols like the percentage sign. Teletype code, which punched holes into tape in five-column units, had been designed to minimize wear and tear by assigning the code combinations with the fewest holes to the most frequently used characters. The code was invented in the nineteenth century by Émile Baudot for a device with five piano-like keys. By 1924 ITA Teletype code for an alphanumeric keyboard included the hash symbol, but the designated position for the hole combination in the tape that meant # might also mean £, because both are "pound" symbols.

As Keith Houston points out in his book *Shady Characters*, the *libra pondo* migrated from being written lb to being written # by the time of Newton.[5] The "L" indicating a Roman unit of weight was transmogrified into a £ to designate the pound sterling of currency. Because # and £ had grown to be very different in meaning, the Teletype hole propagated a false equivalence between numbering items and figuring out their value as a weighted standard. A mistranslation between count and amount became possible. As if there weren't already enough semiotic confusion, to a Russian user of the Teletype the hole combination for "pound" also meant Щ, the "shcha" sound in the Cyrillic alphabet and part of the consonant ending when the word "borscht" is pronounced correctly by a native speaker.

The rationalization about ASCII and the pound sign on the 1968 phone makes sense, but Kerr tells another equally likely story about the star and diamond replacement. According to this version of the substitution decision, attributed to his colleague Lauren Asplund, the # key was preferable because there was no diamond key on standard office typewriters. And Bell Labs designers knew that typewriters would be needed for producing corporate instruction manuals to explain the new telephones to employees.

Although the pound/number sign became a fixture on early typewriters starting in 1878, its location could migrate depending on the model and country of origin. A Blickensderfer typewriter from 1895 located the "#" under the "Q"; a 1905 Royal placed it above the "3," and a Lambert positioned it in 1902 to the right of the "R" in its circular array. The Smith Premier No. 4, which was packed with upper-case and lower-case letter keys, gave "#" its own key to the right of the capital "P." As the symbol became more common on office equipment, so did its ambiguities in pronunciation. A 1917 manual for business arithmetic explained that "#" could mean both "number" when "written before a figure" and "pounds" when "written after a figure."[6]

Once the symbol for the twelve-button phone was decided upon, designers struggled to find a better name. Many disliked the prosaic sound of "the pound key" or "the number key" as designations. These terms were too burdened with traditional weights and measures. They lacked any connotations of the utopian future, which this key for talking and listening machines represented. Some Bell Labs designers, still nostalgic for the enthusiasm of the field tests, lobbied for retaining the name "the diamond key," even though the # symbol looked nothing like a diamond.

By 1968, it would have just barely been possible to call it "the hash key." But at that time only computer programmers would have known about "hash code" or "hashing functions" for mapping data by assigning strings. This kind of high-tech "hash" likely came from the term for food mixed together after being cut into small pieces, from the French word *hacher*, which has the same root as the English "hatchet," although some claim the name for the hash symbol's origins are Germanic, a slurring of "hatch," from the word for a fenced or grated opening, like a medieval portcullis used for protecting castle doorways, which also looks like the latticework of the mark itself.

One of the key's co-inventors, Don MacPherson, wanted to give the hash symbol a name with more flair and romance by introducing the noun "octothorpe" to the world. With eight-points on the symbol "octo" was a sensible choice, but "thorpe" seemed a random appendage. The inside joke at the company was that "thorpe" might be a reference to Jim Thorpe, the beloved Olympian who was born in Oklahoma tribal territory and educated at the Carlisle Indian Industrial School.[7] AT&T customers rejected MacPherson's neologism. The phone was adopted successfully at the Mayo Clinic but the term "octothorpe" was not.

As banks reduced their staffs of human intermediaries, and automated customer service became the norm, the pound symbol became associated with dehumanizing interactions with powerful corporations. Language columnist William Safire noted the difference between "punch"-ing a number rather than dialing it when the consumer was confronted with instructions from a "synthetic-syrupy recorded voice." He associated informational violence with the name of the new telephone key: "pound evokes a mashing of the desired button, as one pounds on a door."[8] Safire acknowledged the existence of the "octothorp" designation but suggested that "gridlet" might be a more likable name for the new key fast becoming demonized. As a pictogram, the gridlet sign might even evoke fond nostalgia for children's games, such as tic tac toe or hopscotch.

In isolation the hash key was limited in its expressive capacities. During the telephone banking transactions that Safire despised, it was mostly used to tell a computer that a sequence of numbers had reached its conclusion and was ready to be processed as data or executed as instructions. However, computers had already begun their transformation from devices for calculation to ones for communication. From the buds of the hash prefix there would flower many appealing fruits, as more people inhabited digital spaces. Like any subsequent chapter in any creation mythology what actually took place around that tree of knowledge depends on one's perspective.

#INVENTOR

Nobody invented the hashtag, although a man named Chris Messina asserted on his website that he was the originator. Reporters have seemed remarkably likely to accept his claim at face value. Some even asked Messina why he didn't patent such a useful invention.

The story goes that on August 23, 2007, Messina sent a message on Twitter asking "how do you feel about using # (pound) for groups. As in #barcamp [msg]?"

Messina's use of the first Twitter hashtag #barcamp cited a term familiar to people in the inner circle of Twitter. BarCamps were popular tech meet-ups that operated like impromptu conferences with mandatory participation. Showing up at a BarCamp meant consenting to its self-organizing structure and expectation for active engagement. At the start of the event the premise was that everyone showed up with something that they wanted to teach and something they wanted to learn. BarCamps were said to be named after a programming slang term "foobar" and were supposed to be the proletarian alternative to the more elitist Foo Camps run by tech guru Tim O'Reilly.

Each syllable ("foo" and "bar") could designate a placeholder variable in a computer program. The compound term "foobar" was obviously a nod to the World War II military acronym FUBAR, short for "fucked-up beyond all recognition," a more arcane variant of the more common SNAFU ("situation normal all fucked up").

If #hashtag is a compound object composed of both the hash symbol and the letters following the sign, #barcamp is a compound compound object. When Messina tweeted #barcamp, he differentiated the "barcamp" brand from all of the possible "bars" and "camps" advertising themselves on Twitter.

What's annoying about Messina's invention story is the fact that hashtags had been used to separate channels on Internet Relay Chat for years. IRC users applied hashtags to designate territory for people with common interests or a shared group identity. For example, the occupants of the #StarTrek group were both science-fiction nerds and programming geeks.

By the time of Messina's tweet in August 2007 rumor had it that hashtags were already in use on another social network that specialized in "lifestreaming." Jaiku, like many millennial social network platforms, is now a defunct company. It began as a Finnish startup before being acquired by Google. Like Twitter, Jaiku was also a microblogging service that limited users to very short status updates.

The Finns' familiarity with hashtags shouldn't have been surprising, because Internet Relay Chat was invented at the University of Oulu in 1988. A display of the first IRC server, which was home to http://tolsun.oulu.fi, has been preserved behind glass at the campus so that visitors making their pilgrimages to shrines in Internet history can see the holy object for themselves.

Twitter had been in use without the handy hashtag rule for over a year when Messina tweeted his suggestion. The company's very first message was from chairman and co-founder Jack Dorsey who announced "just setting up my twttr," at 12:50 p.m. Pacific Time on March 21, 2006. With that utterance Dorsey's first tweet entered the annals of other famous first messages on technology platforms, including "What hath God wrought?" by Samuel Morse for the telegraph and Alexander Graham Bell's "Mr. Watson—come here—I want to see you" for the telephone. Dorsey's tweet could be commemorated in a catalog of similar first messages, which included examples from less famous progenitors, such as "QWERTYUIOP," which initiated the use of ARPANET, or the creepy first AOL instant message "Don't be scared . . . it is me. Love you and miss you" from the company's Vice Chairman Ted Leonsis to his wife.[1]

Less famous is the fourth message on the Twitter platform, which also read "just setting up my twttr." This message was posted four minutes later by a female Twitter employee named @crystal. Although largely overlooked in Internet histories that focus on male software engineers, anthropologist Jennifer Cool has argued that figures like Crystal Taylor, who is currently listed as a "Customer Support Manager" at Twitter, deserve more attention.[2] Cool observes that @crystal opened the third account on Twitter and was the most frequent tweeter in the company's early days. As a designated Twitter support person, Cool sees in Taylor a woman assuming the traditional role of "feminized labor" by offering her services deferentially to more economically important or organizationally assertive individuals.

As an early adopter, Cool was on Twitter close to when it first went live. She joined the service in April 2006, just days after Dorsey and Taylor started tweeting. Using ethnographic methods of participant observation, based on her own years in the tech industry, Cool has analyzed the invention myths of Twitter and has come to conclusions that deflate the founders' self-aggrandizing account of knowing from the start that status updating technologies could initiate momentous changes. Cool learned about the company from her friend Dom Sagolla, who invited her "to test out a 'group send,' SMS application." Three years later Sagolla became the author of one of the first style guides for Twitter: "We as participants can write our own dictionary, tag items and text, and invent a potent new language together."[3]

Although Twitter has posted timelines that present the company as a platform for revolutionary antiauthoritarian change from the start, users were slow to see its utility for airing public sentiments about significant breaking events. In those first months it was difficult for Cool and other early users to see what purpose Twitter was supposed to serve. Some people saw it as a more public form of text messaging, which might be similarly useful for pinging friends or family members with practical information, reminders, or updates.

@crystal mastered the genre of the Twitter aphorism early. In the first months of the site she often posted pithy observations like "corn: it's the new potato" or "I like the word gale . . . too bad it's not used more often." Her frequency of posting was explained by the fact that many of her status updates focused on her weekly routines, such as frequenting happy hours or attending yoga classes. Eschewing depictions of Twitter as a visionary locus of activity that incubated dramatic political rebellions like the Arab Spring, which are now common in hindsight, @crystal characterized her workplace as a site of mundane socializing and frequent lulls. For example, in May of 2006 she writes "the office is so quiet . . . love being here when it's like this."

Messina's specious claim to inventing the hashtag is in keeping with the grandiosity of other origin stories associated with Twitter. Rather than copy the conventional "garage founding" narratives associated with other technology companies, Twitter's inception is supposed to have taken place at a playground near a slide and monkey bars. Accounts by business journalists generally accept the company's public relations story at face value and list South Park in San Francisco as the place the company began.

Before celebrities like Ashton Kutcher and Oprah Winfrey become power users of the site, jockeying to be the first to garner a million followers, the people who used Twitter were mostly people who either worked for Internet technology companies or were interested as journalists, academics, technophiles, computer nerds, or hackers. Twitter's technology often was not able to handle periods of heavy use. Sightings of the Twitter "fail whale" that indicated that the service was down were common in those days.

Using a concept from another anthropologist, Christopher Kelty, Cool has argued that Twitter began serving the needs of a limited "recursive public," which Kelty defines as "a group constituted by a shared, profound concern for the technical and legal conditions of the possibility of their own association."[4] Within this relatively small world, individual expression was less like publishing or advertising and more like conversation. Once hashtags were inserted into these conversations, they became visible to a growing demographic of outsiders. Soon decisions would have to be made about which verbal exchanges would be flagged for special notice and how emerging systems of symbolic categorization would be managed as hashtags became more noticeable to the world.

#PERSON

Jasmeen Patheja sleeps in the park. Not because she has nowhere else to go, but because she is trying to make a point. She is leading a campaign to reclaim public space in Indian cities, particularly for female citizens frustrated by bystander tolerance of pervasive street harassment.

Patheja's feminist collective Blank Noise uses the hashtag #MeetToSleep for their activist slumbering. On Instagram there are otherworldly images showing supine women resting on mats and blankets against a backdrop of lush greenery—sometimes in clumps, sometimes alone. The women adopt a variety of recumbent positions in the tagged photos. One knee up, an elbow over a face, or resting on one side with a top leg flopped over a bottom one. Many of the pictures are from Cubbon Park in Bangalore, where the women are resting in abundant groves of breadfruit, fig, or chestnut. To join the dreaming women, sometimes mothers and daughters come together.

One participant, @mayishahaleema, explains in a tagged video that she came to the event thinking that she would not be able to sleep during the demonstration, but she looked up at trees and the sky and drifted off blissfully. She describes it as "a beautiful experience" that is "so peaceful so relaxing."

The captions for the Edenic scenes on Instagram often echo phrases from Blank Noise's social media presence. Many cite the group's "I never ask for it" catchphrase. Postings also mention the "right to be defenceless."

Even as the women doze blissfully, their awareness of violence is never far away. One of the #MeetToSleep multi-city events was organized to commemorate the fifth anniversary of the 2012 Delhi gang rape that galvanized public opinion into protesting violence against women. Sitting on a blanket on the grass in her Instagram post, poet and sociologist Kamla Bhasin encourages others to join the scene. She reminds viewers "with deepest of sadness" to remember "Jyoti Singh and every girl, boy, and woman who has been sexually harassed in public spaces." Another post discusses "that horrible gang rape and murder of Jyoti" and shows women in Gwalior holding a picture of Singh. The hashtags that accompany the photo include #GwaliorLaunching #MeetToSleep #1BillionRising #RiseResistUnite #RiseInSolidarity #UntilTheViolenceStops #V20IsComing.

Because of the way that hashtags aggregate data, using a proper noun with the name of a previously unknown person is often an effective way to build momentum for a cause. People who are killed prematurely and seen as martyrs are particularly likely to be memorialized in this way. When Michael Brown, an unarmed black civilian, was shot by a law enforcement officer who accused him of shoplifting, #MikeBrown was soon trending on Twitter.

After Nedā Āghā-Soltān, an Iranian philosophy student, died from being shot during 2009 election protests in Tehran, #Neda was used as a digital rallying cry. Although today #Neda is used by the National Eating Disorders Association, the New England Dressage Association, and the Northeast Economic Development Association, at one time it was a distinctive hashtag that deployed one woman's first name to represent resistance to all authoritarian regimes in the Middle East.

Hashtags can also commemorate victims of accidental death. During Ireland's referendum on changing the country's extremely restrictive abortion laws, #Savita became a prominent hashtag that memorialized Savita Halappanavar, a 31-year-old married dentist who died in 2012 from complications of a septic miscarriage; her medical treatment was botched because physicians felt they were legally unable to terminate a pregnancy that was no longer viable. A 1992 incident known as "the X case" involving a fourteen-year-old rape victim forced to carry her pregnancy to term had been less successful at galvanizing pro-choice activists.

This desire to name the victim with a hashtag can be problematic for awareness campaigns about rape or sexual assault. The naming of Jyoti Singh Pandey was particularly controversial. Singh was the 23-year-old physiotherapy student who was abducted with a male companion from a Delhi bus stop in 2012. She was subjected to a night of gang rape and grotesque mutilation on a minibus before being dumped disemboweled at a remote underpass. It was said she wrote the words "Mother, I want to live" on a piece of paper, but medical treatment failed and she died in a Singapore hospital. Before this famous crime, legal, medical, and journalistic norms had contributed to persistently high statistics of unreported and unprosecuted gang rape in India. Until 2008 coverage of rape cases in the news media was actually forbidden, even when identifying information about the victim was not released. The global women's rights movement has done much to ensure that the identities of victims of sexual assault be kept confidential and that names of those accusing perpetrators of rape are not published. However, prioritizing guarding female reputation might do little to dissuade criminal behavior or to change gendered power relations.

Twitter offered a new channel to publicize rape as a widespread human rights abuse, but it also challenged norms about privacy for victims by using identifying hashtags. After the Delhi rape case was first reported, activists adopted several approaches to nomenclature to mobilize and energize participants. Some tagged content with generic subject matter headings, which functioned much like common search terms, such as #DelhiGangRape or #DelhiRapeCase.

Many followed the lead of newspapers and television channels in using pseudonyms to give the victim a proper name without actually identifying her. In an environment of competition for an original scoop, pseudonyms proliferated, including #Amanat, #Damini, and #Nirbhaya. #Amanat is a word for "treasure." #Damini, which means "lightning," is also the name of an avenging heroine in a 1993 Hindi film about gang rape. #Nirbhaya means "the fearless one." Some Twitter users who were extremely eager to participate in all channels of the cultural conversation had to deploy all three hashtags in single tweet that was punctuated with #Nirbhaya #Damini #Amanat. To be read by the widest possible audience, it was necessary to devote more space in the message for metadata.

#Jagruti or "awareness" also became a hashtag for the Delhi rape victim, but because this proper name corresponded to the title of a popular film, this naming scheme invited confusion. Movie fans shared the same hashtag with activists pursuing very different agendas. The same problem emerged for the pseudonym #Braveheart.

Some commentators resisted the rush to rechristen victims as generic figures. As Aryana Banerjee wrote, "no one ever gave me a name like Nirbhaya or Amanat . . . I will never be the nation's pride or the face of women wronged." Others begged media outlets of all kinds to stop what they called the "name game" when subsequent attacks on "Gudiya" (doll) and "Veera" (the brave one) continued the trend of anonymous fame.

After the father of the Delhi rape case victim came forward to identify his daughter publicly, some news outlets still avoided publishing her name. In contrast, there was little hesitation among Twitter users who embraced the #JyotiSinghPandey hashtag in their postings. Tweets around Singh's martyrdom for ending sexual violence such as #ShineJyoti or #JusticeForJyoti soon proliferated. Twitter users even adopted the murdered woman's identity in their user IDs in order to publicize the cause.

It is significant that the Blank Noise activists avoided using any of the most common hashtags associated with the Delhi rape case crime in their social media channels. Some of the #MeetToSleep women did mention "Nirbhaya" briefly in their videos, but they didn't call out the term in the text with its hashtag. Rather than tap into sensationalist coverage of the crime against Jyoti Singh or rely on stock language curated by the Indian media, the women in the parks wanted to use their own language and their own hashtags.

Since 2003 Blank Noise has devoted itself to combating street harassment, which is commonly known in India by the euphemism "eve teasing." As an artist, Patheja's initial project was to document men who made women feel at risk by turning her camera on street harassers. But she soon abandoned her initial shaming strategy in favor of more creative approaches. Today Blank Noise orchestrates social media campaigns coupled with live events. As Patheja described the initiative, Blank Noise was devoted to "building testimonials, creating vocabulary, and creating a safe space for people to be able to talk about their experiences."[1]

Blank Noise volunteers have been encouraged to adopt new identities as #ActionHeroes. They reclaim public space by doing seemingly purposeless activities like idling, loafing, or congregating for no purpose. These are not passive activities. According to Patheja, #ActionHeroes were encouraged to make "eye contact," lean on railings, and generally be "unapologetic about their presence and purpose in city spaces." For example, in "Talk to Me," one of the group's best known public performances, female Blank Noise volunteers sat at five tables in Bangalore's notorious "rapists' lane" for a one-hour conversation opposite a male stranger. The rules were that the pair could discuss anything but street harassment to emphasize the women's humanity rather than issue-oriented political advocacy.

In addition to the #ActionHero and #ActionSheroes tags, volunteers are encouraged to use the #SafeCityPledge tag to designate commitments for everyday participation. Pledges could be eloquently simple assertions, such as "I pledge to walk alone at night."

In their #INeverAskForIt campaign—women provide photographs of the clothing they were wearing when they felt victimized by street harassment. Many have also donated the apparel to Patheja's group for public installations. The neutrality of the garments offers additional evidence of the fact that the women were not instigators of the abuse.

Blank Noise has collaborated on hashtag initiatives with other feminist organizations, such as Delhi-based Breakthrough, which describes itself as "a global human rights organization that uses the power of media, pop culture and community mobilization to inspire people to take action to ensure dignity, equality and justice." According to Radhika Takru, a social media manager for the group, Breakthrough adapted elements from an earlier social media campaign about taking action to prevent violence against women. They emphasized the idea of interrupting an attack with the hashtag #RingTheBell or #BellBajao in Hindi.

Unfortunately such partnering limits the length of messages in common. The use of dual hashtags that recognize the branding strategies of both campaigns, #SafeCityPledge and #RingTheBell, leaves less room for communicating the actual message. Because India is famous for its female-only train cars and bus sections, Blank Noise and Breakthrough have jointly organized events in which women sat in the general compartment on different forms of transportation. In these actions, participants were encouraged to use the unwieldy twenty-character hashtag #SegregationNoSolution.

It is important to note that in the immediate aftermath of the Delhi crime relatively few Indians subscribed to Twitter. Westernized social media platforms were more likely to reflect the biases of the bourgeois concerns of those climbing corporate ladders or clamoring for consumer culture. Furthermore, Hindu nationalists and other advocates for reactionary policies that remove women from the public sphere have embraced the same channels as feminist activists, which can pose challenges for the information workers at Breakthrough and Blank Noise.

Such managing of online messaging involves many kinds of invisible labor in tending social interchanges and instructing users in naming conventions. Staff must steer discussion toward applying the right metadata, shut down those trying to derail meaningful conversation—particularly with counterproductive trolls advocating "men's rights"—and distance themselves from revenge-oriented advocates for the death penalty. After all, not everyone on social media chose to focus sympathetically and sentimentally on the victim of the Delhi rape case. Some Twitter users channeled their hashtag-making to focus wrath upon the accused with hashtags such as #Death4Rape.

Although at present the rise of the so-called smartphone generation in India may be radically changing the media landscape, at the time of the crime most phones in India tended to be lower-tech devices. Despite rapid modernization efforts, many inhabitants of the country remain illiterate, and thus they are less likely to be influenced by channels of text information. As she explained, Takru didn't expect rural villagers to "like our page" in places without electricity or other infrastructural basics, such as reliably clean water. To reach these underserved populations, Breakthrough has used video vans and street performances.

I have seen the bus stop and underpass of the Delhi gang rape crime scenes in person. What I learned from field research about online activism was how little many who gathered in the streets associated the hashtag with their cause. I talked to several young women at Sarai, a research center for Indians studying digital culture. They had gone to the India Gate monument and had joined the mass protests at the central police station. Although the #IndiaGate hashtag was often used with #Nirbhaya and the other pseudonyms, the bulk of their digital discourse was less public. Witnesses from Sarai asserted that it was usually text messages from friends that brought them to the event. As they expressed outrage about the prevalence of gender-based violence, widespread failures by police and other authorities in reporting and prosecuting crimes against women, and poor public safety, they said they also sought more private forms of solidarity at impromptu consciousness-raising sessions where they discussed personal experiences among intimate groups.

The technologies that mattered in the Delhi story of political mobilization were not just those of telecommunication and computer-mediated communication. Anger about the failing transportation infrastructure that left citizens dependent upon itinerant autorickshaws and private buses—as the Delhi victim and her companion were—also galvanized activists. Access to public metro lines and large stations at the intersections of multiple transit trajectories facilitated large-scale protests at India Gate and at the city's police headquarters.

When I visited Patheja for a second time in Bangalore in 2015 she was irritated and frustrated. *India's Daughter*, a documentary by British filmmaker Leslee Udwin for the BBC about the Delhi rape case was dominating the news cycle. The filmmaker had superficially appropriated the basic tenets of Indian feminists but presented their words out of context. She also gave one of the killers and the killers' families and legal teams a generous amount of airtime for repulsive blame-the-victim remarks. When the film was scheduled to appear on television in India, nervous broadcasters pulled the show off the air. Of course, millions watched it on the Internet anyway.

The hashtag #IndiasDaughter was in heavy circulation at the time to publicize the movie. Like #Nirbhaya and #Damini, #IndiasDaughter was another pseudonym for Jyoti Singh. By emphasizing her status as a "daughter" rather than a person in her own right, the film's title and the hashtag strengthened stereotypes about women's childlike relationship to patriarchal authority. We were both aghast at the media spectacle around the director and her eagerness to appropriate Indian culture for her own ends. Despite her British and Israeli background, Udwin appeared in a sari on camera.

Patheja was following the #BritainsDaughter hashtag that publicized how sexual violence was also part of the culture of toxic masculinity in the United Kingdom. Many posted information and anecdotes about the prevalence of harassment, sexualization, and police inaction in Great Britain. Some used the hashtag to focus on defending India's safety record with statistics about sexual assaults relative to other countries. Others ridiculed Udwin's inclusion of perpetrator testimony by posting one-color pie charts that listed possible causes of rape as including "short skirts," "alcohol," "flirty behaviour," "walking alone," "television," and "rapists." (The infographic indicated that only the final factor was worth discussing.)

In certain situations, as participants in a global digital conversation about sexual violence, Blank Noise activists might use hashtags with a victim's name, if use of the naming convention seemed necessary. For example, #Asifa raised awareness of the Kathua rape case in which an eight-year-old girl was abducted, raped in a Hindu temple, and murdered in the Indian state of Jammu. It was a particularly egregious crime in which caste, class, religion, age, and gender all skewed power relations. The victim came from a family of Muslim nomadic shepherds, and her minority community had long been persecuted by Hindu nationalists in the region.

Naming a victim can be powerful for humanizing those affected by a particular policy issue. For example, searches with the #Asifa and #JusticeForAsifa hashtags bring up pictures of her black and blue violated corpse, but they also bring up home videos of the living child singing joyfully and expressing herself as a distinct individual with a capacity for being heard.

In the United States the #SayHerName campaign was intentionally designed in 2015 by the African American Policy Forum to emphasize the personhood of women of color who risk abuse while in police custody. On the group's website the famed feminist theorist Kimberlé Crenshaw asserts that "black women are routinely killed, raped, and beaten by the police" but remain anonymous because "their experiences are rarely foregrounded in popular experiences of police brutality."[2] The #SayHerName hashtag is often combined with hashtags containing the names of the deceased, such as #Justice4PatriciaHill or #AiyanasDreams. The #SayHerName hashtag can also perform historical recovery work by publicizing the otherwise forgotten names of female victims of lynching during the Jim Crow era.

Using the name of a person is a logical hashtag strategy, given the importance of naming discrete people in society and modernity's strong emphasis on disambiguating individuals, which a bureaucratic state requires. Overly generic personal names disrupt the orderly maintenance of voting records, arrest warrants, and pension benefits. At the same time, excessively unique baby naming practices can also cause consternation. The couple who announced the ten p.m. birth of their eight-pound newborn "Hashtag Jameson" were excoriated in British tabloids for parental irresponsibility, even though the posting was likely a hoax or a joke of some kind.

Naming can be a critical ritual for induction into the human community. As part of a virtuous cycle, networks of activists use naming purposively and often perform renaming if necessary. They correct, remind, and model practices around specific digital naming conventions, so a hashtag can achieve the necessary critical mass for public recognition. This otherwise invisible informational labor can be more important than more obvious kinds of rhetorical performance amplified by a megaphone, microphone, or broadcast. #Person hashtags stake their claim to the rights of the self by linking ideas about the autonomy of an individual conscious body to its irreplaceability in the social world, which is signaled by the act of naming. The gap created by the loss of the absent person must be filled somehow.

A site of erasure can become a site of writing. The geographical location where the body of a #Person was lost—executed, assaulted, tortured, beaten, deported, or arrested—can be marked with a #Place hashtag as well. #MikeBrown was killed by police in #Ferguson. A place of trauma can also be a locus to amass political crowds that agitate for more direct and less representative forms of democracy.

#PLACE

At one time Hashtag was a fashionable whiskey bar in central Kiev. The name was not spelled out on its polished granite façade, but insiders knew to look for the # logo in raised marble to find its artisanal cocktails and guest DJs. Such ostentatious obscurity was common among the watering holes of the city, which was known for its hidden bars and speakeasies, including ones only documented on Instagram with the hashtag "mesto kotorogo net"—"a place that doesn't exist." The Hashtag bar had seats for barely a dozen customers, although it was often jammed with hipsters spilling out onto the cobblestone streets.

Andrew Lytvyn, one of the bar's owners, explained that "fashion and passion" inspired the bar's theme. Within its elegant architectural footprint tech entrepreneurs from former Soviet countries shouted over the thumping music to boast of having found the holy grail—a way to monetize hashtags. Of course, hashtags can be difficult to convert into hard currency because hashtags are free pieces of metadata sprinkled at the whim of an individual consumer, often with little regard for financial strategy. How can a company squeeze profit from #FollowMe or #PhotoOfTheDay or #Love? The corporate website for Lytvyn's company Hashtago attempted to explain the magic of "conjunction & disjunction to find value within datasets" that would allow corporate clients to "read social media like a book" from proprietary dashboards.

Those who had mastered the arcane knowledge of spinning hashtags into gold sent out an invitation to ring in 2017 at Hashtag with the beautiful people. The montage of seductive images designed to promote the celebration included popsicle-licking models and a blue-eyed bulldog. A few weeks later the place was shuttered permanently. Unfortunately, there were also less savory stories about the establishment that linked it to the contraband economy of the so-called dark web. The authorities had been eager to see the doors of Hashtag close, and the proprietors were "partying too hard" to keep them open.

There have been other hashtag-named bars in Jaipur, Staten Island, Sofia, and Baku. Each one connects the idea of the hashtag to a physical location somewhere on the globe, a site of conviviality and heady inebriation in which people assemble in real time. Of course, bars are also difficult places to have sustained conversations, especially bars with loud music that adhere to the interpersonal scripts of the one-night stand.

Kiev has many different kinds of public spaces in which people can assemble face-to-face. The present-day Ukrainian capital is organized around bars, parks, coffee houses, malls, and traditional public squares of various sizes and shapes. The Spanish sociologist Manuel Castells, who has studied the strategies of social movements around the world, has argued that the political and cultural functions of "symbolic public space" can be performed either in urban space or in cyberspace and that patterns of participation can fluctuate between these domains.[1] In other words, people often oscillate between the material world of the built environments of cities and the informational world of online networks. For example, a customer could simultaneously appear in the Hashtag Bar and in the screen environment of the smart phone application Foursquare, because users of this mobile app were able to "check in" to the location when mobile devices registered proximity to the physical site on Vozdvyzhens'ka Street. Regulars of the Hashtag Bar could even compete for the title of "mayor" by checking in more frequently than other contenders. In the same way citizens might register their presence in the largest square in the center of the city both by standing on the pavement visible to security cameras and by uploading images to Instagram that are automatically geotagged with their location.

The Hashtag bar had been founded in 2014, the same year that huge crowds had finally succeeded in ousting pro-Russian strongman Viktor Yanukovych after months of public demonstrations and violent clashes. The Software Studies Lab of new media professor Lev Manovich curated Instagram images shared by 6,165 people in central Kiev during the 2013–14 Ukrainian citizen uprisings and discovered that the raw dataset was remarkably heterogeneous. Photos shot by citizen journalists that documented the tumultuous scene in the square were mixed in with text, graphics, and stock images that could come from anywhere. Exterior shots of crowds, encampments, or the buildings that loomed above the protestors were interspersed with domestic selfies and other photos capturing interior locations.

The main protests were held in Independence Square, Maidan Nezalezhnosti. "Maidan" means square in Ukrainian. From their experiences consuming journalism from abroad, many of the demonstrators were well aware of the power of using a place-name as a hashtag. Using a geographical address as metadata alerts others to assemble in a specific place or connect to its occupants remotely. If the hashtag for the location begins to trend on social media, news crews may be more incentivized to cover breaking events there. But activists also wanted to frame their uprising as part of a more universal struggle in the post-Soviet world. To create a hashtag that encapsulated both the specific and the general, participants used #Euromaidan or #Maidan instead of signaling readers with the precise name of the real geographical location in Kiev.

The concept of the public square in its abstract form has become a powerful one for theorizing about digital congregation. Supreme Court decisions about Internet law have explicitly compared digital platforms to the "public square" in arguing for unobstructed access to online services as a civil right. In *Packingham v. North Carolina*, the court ruled that registered sex offenders could not be barred from computer networks because websites are a site of "speaking and listening in the modern public square."[2] In explaining the hands-off role of her country's diplomatic presence in the rest of world, U.S. Secretary of State Hillary Clinton insisted that American policy was opposed to telling "people how to use the internet any more than we ought to tell people how to use any public square, whether it's Tahrir Square or Times Square."[3]

As a location in the real world, Maidan Nezalezhnosti is a place of historical resonances. In 2004 it was the site of the largely peaceful Orange Revolution. Orange revolutionaries used the square as a stage for civil disobedience, sit-ins, and general strikes. They assembled to reject a dominant culture of political corruption so extreme that authorities avoided a thorough investigation when the opposition candidate was mysteriously poisoned by dioxin. Before becoming Independence Square in 1991, the square had been called many different names over a century of solidarity and struggle in heart of the metropolis. It had been Khreshchatyk Square like the broad cosmopolitan boulevard that connected two of its corners. When successive waves of revolutionary fervor toppled the czar it became Duma Square to honor the nearby building where parliamentary procedures of representative democracy were enacted. After bourgeois capitalists were ejected from the government, it became Soviet Square to laud the more radical workers' councils that followed. To solidify the city's ties to Bolshevism it was also called Kalinin Square, a name it resumed after Nazi occupation. The Nazis had liked Duma Square despite installing a puppet regime but had insisted on using the Ukrainian name rather than the Russian one. From 1977 to the breakup of the Soviet Union, it was called October Revolution Square.

Today the main landmark of Maidan Nezalezhnosti stands atop a huge victory column of white Italian marble with a gilded capital. She is Berehynia, a Slavic goddess of protection cast in bronze, holding a branch of roses above her triumphant head. The other monumental presence dominating the square is a message several stories tall: FREEDOM IS OUR RELIGION! Below this declaration in red letters the links of an enormous chain are shown shattering against a blue sky. The exclamation shrouds the gargantuan trade union building that was torched during the #Euromaidan uprisings. From December 2013 to February 2014 it had been the headquarters for antigovernment forces.

The fire was just one of many violent incidents from the heroic to the pathetic associated with the most deadly days of the square. During this tumultuous period, packages labeled "medicine" contained explosive devices, and patients from makeshift hospitals were abducted and tortured. Up the hill from the square snipers had perched and looked down on their civilian targets through telescopic sights. Once the shooting started, corpses were dragged into the lobby of the square's four-star landmark hotel. The desperation that brought people to the square could terminate in morbid consequences that were even more grotesque. A 55-year-old man hung himself from a temporary metal Christmas tree that had been erected in the square as a joyful symbol of the winter holidays. His body was initially obscured by the banners and placards that festooned the structure.

After the traumatic events of 2013 and 2014, the square has returned to its dormant state as a nexus of street fashion spectating, urban caffeination, and underground shopping. The main danger to visitors in the square is probably being accosted by mascots dressed up as big-headed cartoon characters or by con artists accusing good Samaritans of stealing dropped wallets.

Kateryna Kruk remembers much of the #Euromaidan period in disjointed flashbacks. As a political scientist educated in several universities abroad, she had decided to join protestors on the very first day of the gathering, November 21, 2013, after President Yanukovych had reneged on signing an agreement with the European Union promising economic reforms. Her memory was of rain that was likely to doom the demonstration's success. The stakes were high for those on the square, and the demonstrators were well aware that they were not anonymous, especially after repressive laws were passed in January that criminalized civil unrest. "I was 22 back then; I could go to jail for a minimum of 26 years," Kruk recollected, "longer than I had already lived on this earth." She, like most people, was posting to social media in Ukrainian rather than English in the first few days.

Kruk's digital behavior changed on the twenty-fourth. "I was in the eye of the storm," she said, during the first attempted march to the government buildings from the square up the hill to a complex of offices. "I was on the fence, poisoned by tear gas," Kruk said. "I could see police beating people with sticks."

Documenting her impressions of the conflict in real-time was difficult. She had an old Blackberry device without wireless service. So during the uprising, she scribbled her observations of the chaos on pieces of paper and then ran to a nearby McDonalds periodically to take advantage of the free wi-fi. She was also translating social media streams from Ukrainian into English and became an early adopter of the #Euromaidan hashtag, which she abbreviated to #Maidan when she needed to make space in the 140-character lines or felt that time was of the essence for rapid-fire posting.

"The tradition of the word 'maidan' is one of public assembly," Kruk explained. "It refers both to a square and to a gathering of people. I wouldn't use the word 'maidan' for an event that didn't have some political significance. If I was going to the square for a concert, I would say I was on the 'ploshcha' not the 'maidan.'"

Unlike Kruk, Maksym Dvorovy and Vitaliy Moroz were far away from Independence Square when the demonstrations swelled beyond containment. However, their ties to social media kept them closely connected to the protestors and journalists on the square. Dvorovy, a lawyer at the Media Law Institute for the Centre for Democracy and Rule of Law, was traveling to Strasbourg for training. He recounted the surreal experience of being in the Polish mountains in a hostel and watching online as familiar territory transformed into a conflict zone. "Why am I not there?" he asked himself from his remote location.

Moroz was even more distant from the protestors. He viewed the scenes in Kiev from the other side of the Atlantic because he was doing graduate work in journalism in Boston. As the head of the new media department at Internews Ukraine, Moroz was already a savvy user of hashtags. In 2009 he helped launch the #ElectUA campaign as a way to monitor the integrity of Ukrainian elections in real time. His team created other #Elect-related hashtags for specific regions and reprised their hashtag transparency efforts with voting in 2010 and 2012.

Although he was far from home, Moroz's virtual experience of the violence in the square felt very personal. During the demonstrations one of his colleagues was killed in a taxi; thugs shot him in the chest even though he was a journalist. Moroz had been able to join the protesters during the winter break between semesters, but he was far away again as the safety of the situation deteriorated. From this position of powerlessness, he was inspired to use #DigitalMaidan, a new variant of the #Maidan hashtag, to encourage solidarity with the protestors from abroad. In a fast-motion video entitled "How a Twitter Storm Works" Moroz showed how an hour of concerted hashtag deployment with pre-made tweets containing #DigitalMaidan, #Euromaidan, and #Ukraine could publicize human rights and civil society issues and generate buzz as a trending topic.[4]

In the beginning of the demonstration little of the event's online presence was in English, and only a very few used Twitter as a way to record their participation in the demonstrations. Much of the Euromaidan activity was on Facebook, which had only introduced hashtags the previous June as a way for members to follow trending topics. On Maidan's Facebook pages passengers sought rides to the demonstrations, and drivers with vehicles offered them passage. Facebook also served as a clearinghouse for addressing the infrastructural needs of the protestors who required food, fuel, shelter, and medical supplies to sustain their efforts.

When processing metadata about places, Twitter and Facebook may sort information very differently, as Internet scholar Zeynep Tufekci has observed. After the shooting of Michael Brown by the police in Ferguson, Missouri, she noticed that her Twitter feed was full of news from activists about events in #Ferguson. In contrast, she only saw two mentions of Brown's death in her Facebook feed in the hours after the incident. She attributed the difference to Facebook's practice of algorithmic filtering, which privileges content featuring banal status-checking among self-satisfied family and friends over more potentially uncomfortable news about social justice issues. In this way Tufekci argued that the hashtag #Ferguson could affect the geographical place Ferguson.[5] #Ferguson's presence on Twitter might bring people out into the streets to demonstrate, while its absence on Facebook might affect the size and diversity of the assembled crowd.

Using a place-name with a hashtag can also change sites of sanctuary into potential sites of danger. Kruk noted that after the 2015 terrorist attacks in Paris the #PorteOuverte hashtag was intended to alert vulnerable pedestrians about zones to hide in an "open door" building. Others begged those on social media not to write about giving people shelter with the hashtag, not only because faraway observers were "polluting the space" with generic expressions of solidarity, but also because reposting specific locations could allow gunmen to see unlocked addresses where the bloodbath could continue.

In Kiev the same metadata proved not to have the same function on different social networks. #Euromaidan was used differently on Twitter, Facebook, and Instagram. Yevhen Fedchenko, Director of the Mohyla School of Journalism, observed that Russian-language social media platforms like VKontakte (often abbreviated to VK) also played a major role. Such sites were preferred by most Ukrainians during the pre-uprising period. VK and other Russian sites were less regulated by corporate franchises from the West and thus offered more generous access to free pirated entertainment.

Political polarization blossomed on VK during the crisis under the banners of competing hashtags. Pro-Euromaidan activists used the site to promote the cause of Ukrainian nationalism or membership in the European Union. Those who favored maintaining close ties to Russia used the #Antimaidan hashtag to depict the demonstrators in the square as lawless marauders who terrorized innocent people and defiled an otherwise "clean city." Extremists joined the fray, like 22-year-old Maria Koleda, a red-haired, ponytailed young woman whose #Antimaidan social media feed on VK and Instagram was cited by Ukrainian authorities as evidence of her pro-Russian militancy. She was accused of wounding three people with a show weapon that had been altered to fire live ammunition.

Pavel Durov founded VK in 2006 with his brother Nikolai, but he may have been forced out of his own company when he refused to give information gleaned about Ukrainian activists to Russian security services. Eventually VK was banned in the Ukraine as part of an embargo against Russian goods and services in retaliation for the seizure of territory in the eastern part of the country by pro-Russian separatists. However, many get around this digital blockade by using virtual private network (VPN) technologies. In recent years VK has asserted that monitoring hashtags can be important for preserving public health and safety. For example, the platform argues for the right to block accounts associated with "groups of death" hashtags, which aggregate tips for suicide.[6] According to VK's logic, this form of censorship prevents vulnerable young people from taking their own lives.

Just as there were #Maidan and #AntiMaidan hashtag binaries that imagined the occupation of the capital as contested territory, there were competing hashtag campaigns about sovereignty in more remote parts of the country. Anti-Russian and pro-Russian politics played out in the pairing of #CrimeaIsUkraine and #CrimeaIsRussia hashtags. In explaining the popularity of the #CrimeaIsUkraine hashtag, Kruk pointed to the power of a location-based appeal for attention to a specific geographical region. According to Kruk, #CrimeaIsUkraine formulated an "answer" to an imagined question with the declarative power of a slogan. Such arguments of definition make assertions about reality that assume self-evident consensus. Those using the pronouncement #CrimeaIsRussia might contest the definitional groundwork of their ideological opponents.

Hashtag activism was also used to object to Russian custody of prominent Ukrainian citizens held for long periods of time, such as the detained journalist Roman Sushchenko or the jailed filmmaker Oleg Sentsov. A few blocks from Independence Square a building was hung with a large #FreeSushchenko banner. Person-named hashtag activism (like #MikeBrown) might also be coordinated with place-named activism (like #Ferguson). For example, an image of a group of demonstrators wearing black and white jail stripes posing for a visually dramatic sit-in at Times Square was posted with the tags #FreeSentsov, #Сенцов ("Sentsov"), #CrimeaIsUkraine, #NYC, #Крим ("Crimea" in Ukrainian), and #Крым ("Crimea" in Russian).

Attention to the linguistic differences between Ukrainian and Russian could also be significant for understanding the political leanings of a particular hashtag choice. Although most Western journalists and observers would tend to use the #Kiev hashtag for content related to events in the capital, many Ukrainian-language speakers preferred #Kyiv to avoid relying on the Russian-language metadata label that many saw as a legacy of the Soviet past.

The aesthetics of particular images on social media were carefully crafted. Demonstrators wore costumes to parade in the square. People were photographed dressed up as Cossacks or knights. Construction hard hats that offered no serious protection against bullets or Molotov cocktails were also part of the fancy dress. Many of these plastic helmets were decorated by volunteer artists who elaborated their surfaces with flowers, emblems, saints, or symbols, much like the craftwork and color devoted to delicately painted traditional eggs.

Anastasia Taylor-Lind, a photographer, set up a makeshift portrait studio by the barricades where she captured her subjects in their ceremonial armor with a medium format camera against a black curtain. Shots featured men cradling weapons and women bearing flowers for the dead. Taylor-Lind used #Kiev and #Ukraine as hashtags when she returned to the city in 2015 to promote her book. Although she claimed that her aesthetic choices were intended to "remove the dramatic visuals" by deleting "the highly seductive and visual backdrop of fire, ice, and smoke,"[7] the images also removed any sense of a specific geography. Just as she used depoliticized place-names, Taylor-Lind deleted the square as a site of conflict. She removed the unsightly Stalinist and postcapitalist structures that had organized the battles that took place there, much as the markings of a soccer field communicate the rules of the game.

One of the curators from the city's Visual Culture Research Center, the architectural critic Natalia Neshevets, was aghast to see Taylor-Lind repackage her experiences into the clichés of a TED Talk. "What is happening behind the black cloth?" she asked. Like Kruk, Neshevets described the demonstrations as "the moment when I grabbed the smart phone," although "social media was always a minute too late." She was working as a local news producer and "fixer" during the occupation of the square, helping journalists with access, sources, and translation. She remembered how annoyed the visitors from the media were that she didn't have a smart phone, although she had "two usual phones" in excellent working order.

The term "visual culture" has a specific meaning for scholars in academia. It suggests that sight is cultivated as a social practice than represents much more than the physiological functions associated with the organic process of optical reception. In addition to more obvious aesthetic and commercial appeals to an audience's sensibilities structured by museum displays or the layout of an advertisement, the study of visual culture includes examining scientific and legal frameworks that filter what might be perceived as significant.

In other words, critics of visual culture assume viewers are inculcated into seeing specific things, and they are also trained to block out things and render them invisible. In this way everything from an evidence photograph to a medical scan to a frame-grab of online video is seen through the lens of prior education that disciplines how eyes scan the visual field.

As metadata, hashtags also train the eye and set expectations about what to see. For example, many of the Instagram materials that were harvested from Maidan Nezalezhnosti were tagged with the word #Love. The expectation for these images would be that they offer a vision of cooperation rather than conflict, such as shots of egalitarian interactions that convey the positive emotions associated with a leaderless revolution in which everyone participates. Such images might show sharing of resources (like water and fire) on the square, expressions of affection between dissimilar individuals, and the project of mutual support for the needs of a diverse crowd.

Although demonstrators might be self-documenting aspects of the gathering that represented it as peaceful and loving, the total visual record of #Euromaidan was more complex and contradictory than the #Love label. Another VCRC curator, the filmmaker Oleksiy Radynski noted that many of the cameras that came with news crews to cover events were "war machines" as much as they were "media tools." According to Radynski, if Dziga Vertov had ogled the city of Kiev through the "kino-eye" of the twentieth-century cinematic gaze, it was the "kino-fist" described by Vertov's rival Sergei Eisenstein that decimated the fraternity of the twenty-first-century city.

Rather than see the Kiev uprising as a "hashtag revolution" that coalesced around textual metadata, Radynski insisted that it was moving images on YouTube that brought many people into the streets. In his view there were also many squares in the city that became distributed stages for violent performances, additional "scenery for blockbusters," including Bessarabska Square, where a statue of Lenin was toppled from a podium celebrating Russian-Ukrainian cooperation. Radynski's own videos on YouTube avoid romanticizing the political crowd in the square or depicting an undifferentiated expression of the general will as a unified revolutionary mass. In his videos intrusive objects periodically insert themselves in an already divided body politic, thereby marking further divisions between participants. Ambulances, coffins, police shields, video screens, stage barriers, and flaming tires enforce separations. The crowd often breaks and is broken.

The French philosopher Jacques Rancière has discussed the "distribution of the sensible" as fundamental to the apportionment of vital political and aesthetic resources. "Politics revolves around what is seen and what can be said about it, around who has the ability to see and the talent to speak, around the properties of spaces and the possibilities of time."[8] Speaking to a large public audience in Kiev at an event commemorating the fiftieth anniversary of the 1968 barricading of Paris during a dramatic period of unrest orchestrated by a countercultural alliance of French students and workers, Rancière described mass demonstrations occupying public space as a "shortcut" that "dynamically links a local problem to a system of oppression" and thereby bypasses the bureaucratic procedures of representative governments that privilege the hierarchical relationships of command and control.

In many ways hashtags are a mechanism for the *redistribution of the sensible*, by making particular kinds of content more perceptible to potential audiences. Text, images, and video tagged with #Euromaidan can gain visibility by jumping to the top of a user's social media queue. The act of labeling a chunk of data shines a spotlight on it for a heterogeneous audience that may be composed of both activists seeking to reach a critical mass of participants and security forces planning their crackdown on a crowd of unruly dissidents.

It is interesting to note that Taksim Square in Istanbul is named after the word for "distribution" or "division." It was originally a nexus for Istanbul's water collection from the north under the sultanate and a hub for reapportionment of the supply to specific branches of the city. The square has also served as a site that managed other kinds of circulation during its history: the traffic of people and later automobiles, the flow of exchanges of goods in the market economy, and the transit of information among actors in urban space. After all, squares are places to trade gossip and share intelligence, as well as locations for noisy rallies and boisterous speeches. The Taksim Square site also commemorated the founding of the modern Turkish state by being home to the Monument of the Republic, which was unveiled in 1928. The hashtag #Taksim was used to protest the rising authoritarianism of the government of Recep Tayyip Erdoğan and to object to a specific plan for urban renewal that would chip away at the public and secular real estate of nearby Gezi Park and convert the area to uses for private enterprise and religious observance.[9] In Rancière's terms, hashtag activism about Taksim Square should open up a shortcut to get around blocked access to the forces of power and privilege that were making plans to transform the neighborhood.

However, using hashtags in urban spaces could enable another kind of shortcut, one that actually exacerbates existing forms of inequality. Christopher Le Dantec, a professor of "digital civics," has written about "smart cities" that make tools for direct democracy available to urban dwellers through their mobile phones. He argues that these well-intentioned initiatives have a tendency to benefit the haves rather than the have-nots. For example, when input is solicited to build bike paths or fix potholes, the digitally enabled wealthy rather than the poor are more likely to weigh in.[10] Thus hashtags can be a way to jump the line in requesting city services by making some demands seem more urgent than others, because they are more visible to local governments.

The adoption of hashtag practices during the 2013–14 Kiev winter demonstrations was also coopted by many commercial interests. As using hashtags became more common, they also became increasingly likely to be used to promote brands and to market products to consumers. By 2018 there were hashtags all over the window signs and billboards of the city to hype everything from gym memberships to gourmet cupcakes. Place-based hashtags were used to encourage holiday tourism or business investment.

In the recent process of decommunization in the country, which wiped out Soviet symbolism even on historical structures, the purpose-built mining city of Komsomolsk, which had been named after a faction of the Young Communist League, was redubbed as the more poetic Horishni Plavni. The city's euphonious name was celebrated with the #HorishniPlavni hashtag. Photos of civic leaders meeting with manufacturers and investors were tagged with the new appellation, as were pictures of the city's green spaces and scenic bridges over the Dnieper River.

The domestication of the Internet has been key to its success as it takes on the banal functions of home entertainment center, mailbox, and lawn display. Nonetheless, the hashtag remains important for urban denizens and the conflicts that play out in city squares of all shapes and sizes. Like the Parisian *flâneur* wandering the streets of a metropolis as a disinterested pedestrian and bystander, the hashtag tends to be a cosmopolitan resident moving through the physical and virtual public spaces of a nation's capitals.

Although the protestors dispersed from the square years ago, the #Euromaidan hashtag is still being used for a range of purposes on Twitter, including commemorating the dead of Maidan Nezalezhnosti as national martyrs, commenting on political referendums that sanction Russia, promoting photojournalism, and disseminating information about the ongoing investigation into the shootings. Using sophisticated digital tools and a complex assemblage of thousands of digital files, forensic specialists continue to construct 3D models that show who attacked whom—as well as when and where.

Like a footprint left behind at a crime scene, hashtags serve as evidence of what happened years ago. The activities of the protestors at Independence Square can be reconstructed from these traces of #Place messages. However, hashtags can serve as testimony as well as evidence. They may bear witness as a #Slogan as well.

#SLOGAN

A hashtag can *tell people what to do*. It can present an order, request, or instruction. #PrayForOrlando asks the faithful to remember the Florida city that was victimized by a gunman in their devotions. #TakeAKnee urges protest during the U.S. national anthem at sporting events. #StopSeparatingFamilies commands immigration officials to respect the kinship units of the undocumented. #DemandVoterID directs citizens to perform gatekeeping at polling places. #SaveTheNHS begs British citizens to preserve the National Health System. #DisruptAging encourages the elderly to challenge stereotypes. Political conservatives in the United States order their followers to #MakeAmericaGreatAgain and stir the country to alertness with #WakeUpAmerica. #FuckIsis uses an obscenity to will an extremist group into oblivion.

A hashtag can issue a command without specifying a precise activity, as the popularity of the Nike slogan #JustDoIt shows. A single word may be sufficient. #Resist rallies opponents of the Trump administration. The #Leave and #Remain hashtags were used in debates about severing or maintaining Britain's connections to the European Union before its historic 2016 referendum.

Of course, sometimes people do not want to be told what to do and resent not being presented with choices. The certitude of a directive might be ridiculed if the demand seems unreasonable. The hashtag #DressLikeAWoman—paraphrased from a comment by Donald Trump about preferred workplace attire for women—was paired with pictures of female astronauts, surgeons, and legislators. #TellDaveEverything sarcastically suggested sharing personal secrets directly with a British Prime Minister who supported government-run surveillance efforts.

A hashtag can also *tell people with more subtlety what to do*. It can suggest a seemingly reasonable way to think and feel about the world. It can present definitions, comparisons, and theories about causality as though these logical suppositions should be treated as unquestioned premises. For example, a hashtag can assert a positive affirmation about equivalency (#LoveIsLove), worth (#UnbornLivesMatter), or acceptance (#RefugeesWelcome). Hashtags can also insist upon basic conditions in negative terms. #NotInMyName renounces political violence in India. #NoBillNoBreak is an ultimatum about gun control legislation coming to the chamber floor. #NoJusticeNoPride adopts a similar template to insist that LGBT basic rights must be addressed before being coopted by feel-good "pride" celebrations.

Most importantly, a hashtag can assure people that they are *connected* to other people. A hashtag affirms that a communication channel is open, that being heard is possible, and that an interdependent web of social ties between equally viable nodes can be made visible for navigational purposes when necessary. A hashtag promises that the preconditions for amplifying a collective signal have come into existence.

This is why expressions of solidarity are often so important for hashtag slogans. Critics may denigrate such purely affirmative gestures as empty acts of "clicktivism" or "slacktivism" with no long-term political impact, but the call-and-response structure that magnifies a hashtag's impact represents more than simple repetition of the same idea. Obviously few hashtags explicitly take the form of a question, such as #WhereAreTheChildren or #AreWeEurope. Yet any hashtag always poses a question awaiting an answer from the audience. The question that the hashtag asks is "are you listening?" or "are you there?"

In addition to providing metadata that allows computers to sort through online conversations more efficiently, hashtags with slogans are speech acts that use language to attempt to bring a new order into existence. Academics use the term "speech act theory" to explain the power of words to perform actions. A Latin vocabulary exists for categorization: "illocutionary" speech brings what it states into being, while "perlocutionary" speech sets a series of events in motion as a way to effect change. According to the speech act theorist J. L. Austin, the former draws attention to the speaker's deeds, and the latter the activity of the audience.[1]

Such word combinations don't just describe the world or comment upon it; they actually transform the world, like a magic spell that can reshape reality with a simple incantation. The classic examples of performative speech acts are legal declarations, such as pronouncing a couple man and wife or a person innocent or guilty at the end of a trial.

Judith Butler uses the example of a doctor announcing "it's a boy" or "it's a girl" upon the occasion of a baby's birth as a speech act with profound consequences.[2] Butler insists that gender is not a fixed biological category; rather gender is an interpretation of a social script that is acted out for audiences. The words of the obstetrician or midwife may set the stage, but other actors including the baby have important roles to play. Each promise, excuse, or recitation of a creed can reconfigure the child's initial gender or challenge its stability.

In other words, every time I am addressed as "sir" I must make a decision about my gender. If I correct the person, I may be expressing my indignation, but I also am expressing my gender. If I don't correct the person, I may be performing my politeness, but I am also performing my gender.

Butler has a theory of performance for political demonstrations as well that assumes that exercising assembly may be more important than exercising speech. According to Butler, when today's masses congregate in the streets, the precarity of their bodies becomes visible. By appearing in public together, demonstrators also resist dominant ideologies of self-sufficiency, personal responsibility, and individual enterprise. They announce themselves as a plural rather than singular political body. For Butler, these acts of assembly do not depend on verbal utterance. A silent candlelight vigil may speak volumes.

Hashtag slogans may contain speech acts that seem similar to the chants heard at live protests, but they operate in another register as well. Because they are aggregated for searching and browsing, hashtags *gather* in online environments. They have a quantitative as well as qualitative existence. If search algorithms and communication platforms facilitate their appearance, hashtags enter the space of visibility. Using Butler it is possible to argue that hashtags perform the work of assembly as well as the work of speech.

The "we" of a hashtag slogan expresses this plurality, whether the compact of unity is enacted explicitly with plural first-person pronouns like "we," "us," or "our." #BringBackOurGirls universalized the outrage felt by many Nigerians—and citizens around the world—after 276 female students were abducted from the Chibok Government Secondary School by Muslim fundamentalists. After #BringBackOurGirls went viral, Nobel Prize-winner Malala Yousafzai, First Lady Michelle Obama, and even the pope used the hashtag to shame the kidnappers, as well as the political leaders who had allowed their radicalized armies to grow unchallenged.

"Girls" can be agents as well as possessions in a plural hashtag slogan. The #GirlsLikeUs hashtag was started by transgender activist Janet Mock to promote positive visibility for transgender women. As hashtag scholar Moya Bailey explains, participants used #GirlsLikeUs to discuss "everything from the desire to transition and the violence of being outed in unsafe situations" to "the banality of everyday living and dreams of job success."[3]

Many hashtags signal shared investments, no matter the grammatical construction, if the call to action requires joint effort. For example, "standing with" is a gesture of solidarity. #WeStandWithParis, #WeStandWithBrussels, and #WeStandWithBerlin express camaraderie with cities that have experienced terrorist attacks. Similarly, #IStandWithPlannedParenthood imagines a stance of collective defense that assumes others will take the side of a U.S. reproductive rights organization, and #IStandWithSurvivors announces a firm commitment to join rape survivors braving adversarial legal processes or attempts to shame them into silence. In these cases, the "I" of personal accountability represents a pledge to membership in the "we" of a communal movement.

There is a famed scene in the 1960 Stanley Kubrick movie *Spartacus* in which the hero is at risk of being crucified by the Roman authorities for fomenting rebellion among the enslaved. First one by one, and then in a cacophonous whole, men rise to declare, "I am Spartacus." This hides the identity of their leader in a display of mass allegiance. In much the same way, users of the hashtag #JeSuisCharlie (or #IAmCharlie) assume the identity of the satirical weekly *Charlie Hebdo* to demonstrate solidarity with the twelve people killed in the magazine's Paris offices in 2015 by Islamic radicals and to proclaim a common commitment to free speech.

The #MeToo campaign has encouraged women from many different walks of life to share their experiences of harassment, assault, discrimination, and marginalization. U.S. news organizations began publishing accounts in 2017 about how Hollywood mogul Harvey Weinstein routinely sexually terrorized would-be starlets, female personnel, and potential employees of his studio. These stories that had long been silenced by nondisclosure agreements and a culture of complicity were aired, and dozens came forward to accuse Weinstein of abusing his position.

In October 2017, to shift attention from perpetrators to victims, actress Alyssa Milano posted "If you've been sexually harassed or assaulted write 'me too' as a reply to this tweet" above an image that read:

Me Too.

Suggested by a friend: "If all the women who have been sexually harassed or assaulted wrote 'Me too.' as a status, we might give people a sense of the magnitude of the problem."

Overnight #MeToo messages flooded Twitter, Facebook, and Instagram in response to Milano's call. The movement spread from the entertainment industry to many other culturally influential fields: publishing, the art world, the restaurant industry, politics, and academia. Like #BlackLivesMatter the metrics on the hashtag were dramatically larger in scale than most hashtags and maintained impressive staying power.

The initial viral spike observable in the United States for the #MeToo hashtag soon was replicated in the data about social media trends from other Anglophone countries. #MeToo was also translated into multiple languages or adapted for foreign audiences. In China the homophone "mi tu," represented by the emojis for "rice" and "bunny," was used to get around the nation's censors who might be searching for dissident content. In France an open letter critical of the movement from successful show business figures called it by its English name rather than #MoiAussi. As a testament to its popularity and brand appeal, by January of 2018 #MeToo had a custom emoji that appeared automatically if Twitter users inserted the hashtag. The image was intended to be three hands from people of different races, although at a distance the symbol appeared to many to be a picture of female genitalia.

As the #MeToo hashtag exploded, black feminists were understandably irritated to see all the attention going to white women. Those objecting to cultural amnesia reminded white feminists that in 2006 Tarana Burke had founded a "Me Too" campaign against sexual assault based on bearing witness to the repetition of individual experiences of violence against women. Burke had used an older social network platform, MySpace, as her main vehicle for spreading the word and building community. When *Time* magazine devoted its cover to "The Silence Breakers" as its "People of the Year" for 2017, white female celebrities like Ashley Judd and Taylor Swift were depicted as the primary faces of the movement and Burke's absence was noted by many.

Another factor explaining Burke's relative anonymity was her choice to develop the "me too" concept on social media without stamping it with the #MeToo hashtag. A search of the Twitter archive shows Burke using the hashtag to curate other kinds of conversation about solidarity in the years before the Weinstein scandal broke. For example, in December of 2010 Burke tweeted about her affection for classic novels about the lives of young women. "@krysilove What? Who wrote it? I just bought my daughter the whole Jane Austen series bc she LOVED Pride & Prejudice. #metoo ;-)"

In Burke's first few years on the platform, her Twitter presence was more likely to utter "me too"—without the hashtag that made the phrase famous—usually in contexts that had nothing to do with sexualized abuse, such as asking questions about the Twitter interface. ("When I reply to people the @ comes up, but do they have to follow me too in order to see my reply?") Her pre-2017 use of "me too" was usually part of an exchange with a specific interlocutor as Burke became a fluent user of the Twitter platform to perform many kinds of rhetorical work.

> @Bassdiggitydawg Kaia used to do that . . . now it's always something that ails her—"ma, I have a pain in my back" I'm like "me too—you"
> @putyrdreams1st You saw Brooklyn's Finest last night? Me too! What did you think?
>
> @Monalisa7872 (me too!! Who knew, lol) RT @ cosmobaker "No worries"—that's some weird shit that white people say . . .

[ME TOO!] RT @writeli:"I'm gonna yield myself the balance of the time."—I'm going to say that at work meetings, but as soon as they start.

Burke's "me too" assertions cover many different kinds of expressions of solidarity, from empathizing with bodily discomfort to sharing frustration about white privilege. Each use of "me too" shows her social awareness about the value of validating common experiences in the task of online community building.

In other words, Burke can legitimately claim to be an inventor of the "me too" slogan long before #MeToo was born, and her work building online community modeled the performative work of the slogan. "It wasn't built to be a viral campaign or a hashtag that is here today and forgotten tomorrow," Burke told a reporter from *Ebony* magazine. "It was a catchphrase to be used from survivor to survivor to let folks know that they were not alone and that a movement for radical healing was happening and possible."[4] Granted, she didn't conceive of her use of the phrase as a machine-readable chunk of metadata, but her understanding of the conditions needed to build trust between victims in the context of a shared conversation was in many ways more sophisticated than merely launching a trending term on Twitter.

#ImWithHer, the hashtag slogan of 2016 U.S. Democratic candidate Hillary Clinton, attempted to ride the wave of hashtag feminism that predated #MeToo. The slogan was launched in 2011 by campaign brand managers. It picked up momentum on social media as a hashtag in 2015 after pop star Katy Perry posted an #ImWithHer selfie on Instagram with Clinton. Tepid voter enthusiasm was signaled by the more ambivalent use of #GuessImWithHer, which eventually devolved into the humorous tag #GirlGuessImWithHer, which riffed on popular "Hey Girl" memes.

Online assertions of feminist cohesion can also easily become vexed by identity politics. Obviously, hashtags with solidarity slogans exclude as well as include, because declaring you are "with" one side suggests that you are inevitably "against" another side. Furthermore, claims of unanimity—particularly about gender relations—are inevitably contested, as the 2014 battle between women waving the banner of #INeedFeminism and those charging ahead under the rival flag of #IDontNeedFeminism demonstrates.

The symmetry of solidarity hashtags is not always what it appears to be, as in the case of #NotAllMen and #YesAllWomen. In 2013 Twitter user @sassycrass parodied a classic contrarian "mansplainer" in a tweet that soon went viral.

> ME: Men and boys are socially instructed to not listen to us. They are taught to interrupt us when we- RANDOM MAN: Excuse me. Not ALL men.

As this posting indicates, the #NotAllMen hashtag was created to satirize men who wanted to be shielded from critique. (#NAMALT for "not all men are like that" is another variant of #NotAllMen.) However, #NotAllMen was also used defensively by men themselves when they wanted to be exempted from blanket criticism about male privilege or female oppression. For example, #NotAllMen has been used to tag videos about the supposed "war on boys" in primary school education.

In 2014 #YesAllWomen began trending among outraged feminists after the shooting of three women at a sorority house in Isla Vista, California, by a 22-year-old professed misogynist. #YesAllWomen expanded to a broader campaign publicizing other examples of feminicide, rape culture, toxic masculinity, violence rooted in male entitlement, and everyday gender discrimination. Discussion of the hashtag was contentious and was resented by many men. So-called "men's rights" advocates on Twitter, such as Single Man Magazine or The Meninist, began angrily using the #YesAllWomen hashtag with derogatory terms like "bitch" and hashtags like #FeminismIsCancer.

Many solidarity hashtags represent political choices as binary, as though the categories of the privileged and the oppressed never overlap. These tensions are best epitomized by the bitterly ironic slogan #SolidarityIsForWhiteWomen, which galvanized black feminists who were exhausted by what they saw as the patronizing, dismissive, or self-aggrandizing stances of white feminists that were adopted at the expense of their nonwhite sisters. This hashtag draws attention to the problem of claiming one affirmative identity category (feminism) without acknowledging how practices of exclusion are tied to more problematic identity categories (racism). The hashtag calls out how the inclusiveness of solidarity in defending a perceived ally could ignore the pain of those relegated to the positions of outsiders.

Mikki Kendall created the #SolidarityIsForWhiteWomen hashtag. As a writer based in Chicago, she has also produced prose in longer formats, such as essays in the *Guardian* and the *Washington Post*. She contributed to the book *Here We Are: Feminism for the Real World*, scripted a graphic novel about online bullying, and penned lesbian steampunk fiction as well.

Kendall launched the hashtag to air her frustration about how Hugo Schwyzer, a self-described "male feminist" and photogenic professor, had continued to be a contributor to popular feminist blogs despite what seemed to be a sordid personal history of online misogyny directed against women of color.[5] Schwyzer's repugnant resumé allegedly also included intimate partner violence, unconditional celebration of pornography and sexual objectification, drug abuse, and sexually predatory behavior directed at his community college students. Yet Schwyzer was defended online by white feminists even after a spectacular public meltdown on Twitter when he confessed to be "awful" to women of color because they "were in the way." Kendall was exasperated by how willingly white female bloggers offered their sympathies as Schwyzer wrestled with his demons while seemingly giving little consideration for the black victims he had appeared to have attempted to intimidate and humiliate.

As Kendall's hashtag attracted users, Schwyzer felt compelled to defend his white feminist defenders. "This whole #solidarityisforwhitewomen thing is an abusive cudgel to be used against a lot of people who are really working at inclusivity," he lamented. Such circling of wagons seemed to prove Kendall's point, that for the privileged solidarity is a fashion statement rather than a commitment to fight oppression more generally, as superficial as donning apparel with the Solidarność logo. For Kendall, their slogans were nothing but easy-to-consume brands.

#BRAND

The post accompanying the photo of the elegant blond woman in white striding off the plane had very few words that were not hashtags:

> Great #daytrip to #Kentucky! #nicest #people #beautiful #countryside #rolandmouret pants, #tomford sunnies, #hermesscarf, #valentinorockstudheels #valentino #usa

In addition to standard hashtag practices for getting a message noticed, like tagging places with proper nouns (#Kentucky), generic nouns like "people" and "countryside" were turned into hashtags, as were common adjectives like "nicest" and "beautiful." Because the Instagram photo-sharing platform allows users to add up to sixty hashtags, this accretion of multiple hashtags to describe an image on the photo-sharing site wasn't particularly strange.

What most seemed to irritate the woman's Instagram audience was the cascade of brand names and luxury compound objects that she tagged, particularly since the woman identifying the expensive designers she was wearing was Scottish actress Louise Linton, the wife of a cabinet official in the Trump administration, who was shown deplaning behind her. Many were offended that the spouse of the United States Secretary of the Treasury, who was supposedly traveling on official business, would so ostentatiously adopt the hashtag-heavy diction of a lifestyle blogger bragging of a shopaholic haul.

Minutes later @emily.e.dickey wrote back to Linton "Please don't tag your Hermes scarf. Distasteful."

@jennimiller29 decided to use a hashtag to register her own disapproval of Linton's display of conspicuous consumption: "Glad we could pay for your little getaway #deplorable."

Linton responded to this criticism of her hashtagging with vitriol. Where there was a proliferation of hashtags before, now there was an efflorescence of emojis to accompany a message that was equal parts sarcasm, entitlement, and self-pity:

Aw!!! Did you think this was a personal trip?! Adorable! Do you think the U.S. gov't paid for our honeymoon or personal travel?! Lololol. Have you given more to the economy than me and my husband? Either as an individual earner in taxes OR in self sacrifice to your country? I'm pretty sure we paid more sacrifices toward our day 'trip' than you did. Pretty sure the amount we sacrifice per year is a lot more than you'd be willing to sacrifice if the choice was yours. You're adorably out of touch. Thanks for the passive aggressive nasty comment.

Linton's acerbic exclamations and rhetorical questions were punctuated with the Heart Eyes emoji, the Muscle emoji, and two Kissing Heart emojis.

Because of the apparent insensitivity of Linton's snarky response, what had been a minor story about misuse of social media soon became a major story about abusive conduct on the Instagram platform and the tone-deaf entitlement of the financially privileged.

The next day Linton publicly apologized, deleted the post, and made her Instagram account private. The brands Linton had trumpeted with her hashtag-heavy prose were eager to distance themselves as well. Spokespeople from Valentino and Tom Ford attested to *Women's Wear Daily* that Linton had not been encouraged to promote their labels with either endorsement deals or free merchandise.

Although the practice of using hashtags to advertise corporate products and services has now become common, during the early months of the hashtag on social media such name-brand promotion was relatively rare. In early 2008 when a famous producer of athletic apparel introduced a highly touted activity tracker for amateur athletes, few attempted to use hashtags on Twitter to generate more buzz.

But just as proper names of people like celebrities have a tendency to trend on social media sites, proper names of brands like Chanel or Adidas can be aggregated for search purposes by hashtags. Sometimes brands launch slogan campaigns to enhance their corporate identities that can have a life separate from the associated brand name, as in the case of #EverythingIsChemistry launched by the cleaning products company SC Johnson and the #LikeAGirl empowerment campaign for young women, which was promoted by the sanitary pad manufacturer Always.

Luxury brands are particularly likely to be associated with the name of a particular designer. The longer history of how merchandise has been identified with the name of a person can be useful for understanding hashtag use for today's brands. Over two thousand years ago, during the time of the Roman Empire, a glassmaker—who was either Lebanese or Phoenician—decided to affix his name to his fragile and intricately wrought wares. These pieces were marked with the phrase "made by Ennion," which was spelled out in raised Greek letters, either on a plaque with dovetail-shaped handles or within a simple rectangular frame. Some vessels had another inscription, which was either an alternative to the "made by Ennion" label or an addition to it. The tagline translated as "may the buyer be remembered." The customer was expected to fill in the rest of the slogan ". . . by the gods."[1]

Two millennia later a few dozen pieces of Ennion's mold-blown glass survive. One of his remaining flasks is rich azure. A clear bowl is covered with geometrical shapes. Other surviving items include an amber-colored pitcher, a topaz-colored two-handled cup, and a bottle with swirling stripes in black, white, and blue. Perhaps the brand name made the objects more obviously precious and worthy of being preserved as they traveled around the Mediterranean.

Before the eighteenth century most paintings lacked titles in the modern sense, although adding a signature to a masterpiece came much earlier, as painters imitated the habits of artisans. From Sophilos imprinting his name into Greek pottery in the sixth century BC to Raffaello Sanzio's signature flourish added to the painting of *The Mystical Marriage of St. Catherine* around 1499, creative professionals experimented with different ways to identify their works, including using symbols or other cryptic non-textual means.

However, brands might be unable to speak for themselves. Modern marketing executives know that their carefully crafted and rigorously tested proper names for corporate identity still need human ventriloquists. Royal endorsements might be considered the first example of this practice of seeking brand ambassadors. Josiah Wedgwood and Sons, manufacturers of eighteenth-century china and porcelain, hawked their jasperware, basaltware, and caneware by celebrating the company's status as "Potter to her Majesty." Wedgwood produced a cream-colored tea set for King George III's wife, Queen Charlotte, and Wedgwood creamware rapidly became known as Queensware, which signaled the product's noble pedigree to enterprising commoners with aspirational ambitions. Wedgwood advertised his sales to aristocrats and named specific pieces for individual members of the royal family. You can still buy flowerpots from

Wedgwood stamped with the "Devonshire Ducal Coronet and Snake" and inscribed with Lady Burlington's signature.

Guides to promoting products with hashtags similarly counsel the strategic use of "influencers" who can use their celebrity—no matter how modest—to animate brand preferences for those who are emulating the lifestyles of the Internet famous. Alice Marwick dubbed these approachable not-quite-celebrities who are only Internet famous "micro-celebrities." In her book *Status Update* Marwick details the rigors of their intense image management practices and 24/7 engagement with fans.[2]

Building on new methods for Internet research, Crystal Abidin has conducted years of in-depth study observing the online habits of the glamorous female influencers of Singapore. These influencers are known for their abundant closets, patronage of plastic surgeons, and tendency to "spam a whole lot of hashtags" on Instagram. For example, a photo of ThyDowager (Peggy Heng) in headphones spinning records at a club is ornamented with #djdowager #modeldj #igsg #sg #grandhyatt #martinibarsg #fdj #djane. Although it might be easy to dismiss influencers as hedonistic exhibitionists with little political clout, Abidin points out that government officials have enlisted them for major public relations campaigns. Politicians have even emulated their techniques to stay in the good graces of the citizens of the island nation.

In the world of Singapore influencers a hashtag may no longer function in its expected role as an easy-to-find archival label, especially when the online environment has become supersaturated with competing information. Such a hashtag must perform more complex kinds of rhetorical work than merely filtering out noise to maintain the interest of its followers. A hashtag might even make itself scarce rather than numerous, hidden rather than prominent, to enhance its rarity as a prized object.

According to Abidin, "influencers decided that they had to gamify hashtags, to make them transient." To exploit common anxieties about FOMO (fear of missing out) among digital multitaskers, Singapore influencers created complex games of hide and seek. For example, #HashtagA might seem to be on the cusp of trending, but an influencer decides to insert #HashtagB to introduce "magic and secrecy." By the time that #HashtagA fully rises to visibility in the popular consciousness, insiders have already migrated to #HashtagC, if they have followed the clues provided by a route of what Abidin calls "subhashtagging." Then the meandering path from #HashtagD to #HashtagE can include intentionally diverging or occluded breadcrumbs across forums or blogs that are not hashtaggable, which leave bait for only the most loyal devotees or virulent haters. Abidin claims influencers often maintain a pose of detachment in dropping these trail markers, thereby transferring attention to the followers who are scrambling to keep up with the constantly receding desired fetish object.[3]

A hashtag may become so rarified that it can only serve as an object for the influencer's own use. When pink-haired Xiaxue (Wendy Cheng) pretended to be interested in running for the legislature, she was the only person who used #XiaxueForNMP. For influencers who don't depend on sponsorship deals, like the socialite Jamie Chua, a flight attendant who married a wealthy Indonesian passenger, the rules of hashtag use are even more idiosyncratic. Chua sprinkles her globe-trotting posts with hashtags that are only intended to be used once, and only by Chua herself, such as #TheLuminousOneGoesToFlorence or #TheLuminousOneGoesToLakeComo. By association, these hashtags might seem to promote her Luminous1 line of skincare products, but the hashtag #Luminous1 is only sporadically used, and never on Chua's own account.

As members of the class near the top of the social media hierarchy, Singapore influencers need to project authenticity to maintain their trustworthiness, even if they also obviously construct elaborate façades to enhance their public appeal. By this logic selective disclosures of imperfection and fallibility can make an influencer seem more "relatable" to her audience. Each faux pas contributes to the perception of a more authentic performance and thereby conveys that the influencer is a more credible arbiter of taste not beholden to sponsoring companies. Abidin describes how influencers may use "snark, counterdiscourse, or paralanguage" that seems at odds with a corporate agenda of selling products. For example, an influencer may display a Gucci bag that is appropriately hashtagged with the designer label, but the influencer might also include hashtags for "a rival brand or knock-off brand" to demonstrate independence.

In the lifecycle of an influencer's career, elaborate rituals of leaving the profession become expected. An influencer may declare a hiatus from taking up endorsements in response to a life event like "a failed romance, a pregnancy, a struggle with finance or coupling," or the daunting prospects of a move or setting up a new household. An influencer may announce that she is undergoing an existential crisis and express her intentions to jettison glitz and glamor and abandon her former obsessions with "metrics and face." An influencer may insist on areas for privacy separate from those of showmanship.

Abidin recounts how an influencer may proclaim an elaborative exit narrative. She may assert that online life has become too toxic and very conveniently embrace a more wholesome lifestyle narrative centered around wellness, mindfulness, self-help, and yoga that is seemingly less commercial and more down-to-earth with more subtle pitches for her merchandise. Even while ostentatiously departing, the influencer remains a micromanager in the economy of digital sentiments. Some make the cynical decision to deflect attention to children or what Abidin calls "micro-micro-celebrities." Others adopt a stance of entrepreneurship and transform themselves into managers of other micro-celebrities, because they "know they are growing old." In other words, it is often the brand of the human spokesperson that ultimately matters most, whether she is peddling a Louis Vuitton bag or promoting travel to Poland, and she must preserve the value of her personal brand through a process of constant reinvention.

In contrast, brands with activist genealogies may be disseminated without celebrity endorsements. There are currently over sixty registered works for "Black Lives Matter" in the U.S. copyright office, including visual materials, sound recordings, and dramatic works. There are twenty-seven entries for copyrighted works entitled "Occupy Wall Street." In both cases, however, the transformation from a popular slogan to an established brand was not immediate. Viral campaigns might seem to take off like a rocket, but before the launch there is always a period of pre-testing and false starts.

#ORIGIN

Before there was #BlackLivesMatter, there was #BlackLife Matters, and before there was #OccupyWallStreet there was #OpESR.

Many were drawn to the Occupy movement against financial inequality by the iconic black and white poster with the headline "What Is Our One Demand?" showing a dancer in a leotard performing an arabesque atop the bronze *Charging Bull* statue that is a landmark of the New York financial district. Behind the ballerina's sinuous pose ghostly gas-masked figures are barely visible. The scene is positioned above three lines of text: #OCCUPYWALLSTREET SEPTEMBER 17TH. BRING TENT.

Zuccotti Park opened near Lower Manhattan's financial district in 1968 and was heavily damaged in the September 11 attacks of 2001. Because of its proximity to Wall Street and its legal status as a Privately Owned Public Space (POPS) not subject to city park curfews, it was a desirable location for the demonstration. The Occupy encampment in Zuccotti Park became the focus of media attention in the city for several weeks. Celebrities mingled among the crowd that included local activists, students, labor organizers, and artists, along with the disabled and the homeless. A few months earlier Operation Empire State Rebellion had also planned to protest Wall Street influence, but only four people showed up ready to camp in Zuccotti Park on the appointed day. Despite being promoted by the online group Anonymous, #OpESR proved to be a far less effective slogan.[1]

Under the banner of "Black Life Matters" more than five hundred "freedom riders" traveled to Ferguson, Missouri, to protest the shootings of unarmed African Americans by law enforcement. The authorities alleged that Michael Brown had shoplifted a box of inexpensive cigars, and he had resisted being taken into custody. The prior existence of a Black Life Matters organization that had produced videos objecting to high levels of gun violence in Chicago seemed likely to generate message confusion, and so the plural #BlackLivesMatter became the permanent tag.

The genealogies of social movements tend to be contested, but one of the widely acknowledged #BlackLivesMatter founders, Alicia Garza, posted "a love letter" to Facebook in 2013 that emphasized the movement's plurality. At the time activists were dispirited by the acquittal of George Zimmerman, who had shot Trayvon Martin in 2012. Her eloquently simple message emphasized the centrality of care and repair: "black people. I love you. I love us. Our lives matter." Her friend Patrisse Cullors reposted Garza's message to Twitter, where it went viral. #BlackLivesMatter became the definitive hashtag that would be used tens of millions of times. The hashtag was associated with Garza's commitment to a queer intersectional womanist politics that had disinvested itself from the politics of respectability.[2] In turn #BlackLivesMatter spurred retorts like #BlueLivesMatter, which defended police officers interacting with suspects, and #AllLivesMatter, which undermined any focus on systemic racism by using an undifferentiated solidarity hashtag asserting blanket unity.

Both of these seminal hashtags became so successful that they could be shrunk to acronyms and still be recognizable to their users in the truncated forms of #OWS and #BLM.

#INTERSECTION

You can visit Cairo's Tahrir Square in a California digital studio. By wearing a virtual reality headset at the University of California, Santa Barbara, a visitor can explore an unpeopled terrain of pavement, lampposts, and monolithic concrete buildings at the heart of the Egyptian capital. In this computer-generated simulation, the thousands of civil servants doing bureaucratic work behind Soviet-style façades are invisible, as are the tourists peering at exhibits in the antiquities museum, and the streets that feed into the enormous boulevards of the city are vacant as well. This exotic electronic world looks like a depopulated sci-fi dystopia as the user's field of vision pans around the empty environment of the 3-D replica. But if a few words are tapped into a handy cell phone using the right hashtag, letters will appear suspended in the virtual space.

Hashtag scholar Laila Shereen Sakr has been creating new ways to navigate social media streams for a number of years. Her data visualizations can look like cloudlike auroras representing constellations of informational activity or groves of surrealistic trees branching around a video-game character at ground level.

During the 2011 Egyptian revolution that overthrew longtime president Hosni Mubarak, the hashtag #Tahrir was used to mark messages about the demonstrations taking place in the main square in central Cairo. Sakr points out that *tahrir* means "liberation" in Arabic, and thus #Tahrir references both a place-name and a slogan. Like other squares in other cities, Tahrir Square reminds demonstrators of other social movements in the country's past. According to Sakr, the site was already historically significant because of its role in the 1919 revolution against British colonialism and was also associated with famed feminist Huda Sha'arawi, who organized conventions of women seeking suffrage and emancipation. Sakr described Tahrir as "an index of the Egyptian people whoever they are" in their struggles against despots. As such, users of the #Tahrir hashtag understood that it was "more than just a place. It is a history that makes us draw the history."

Naming conventions for places in the Middle East often provide important clues about ideological leanings. Sakr argued that place hashtags were often loaded with meaning.

> If someone uses #KSA—Kingdom of Saudi Arabia—you know the person is a royalist. It's an acronym used by wealthy elites and businessmen. #Saudia or #SaudiArabia may have different connotations. And it matters if someone uses Arabic characters rather than English ones.

In other words the topography of imagined community depends not only upon who is drawing the map but also who is using particular naming conventions.

As an anchor for a hashtag's reference point, dates serve a similar function as places. According to Sakr, "In the Middle East in general we always use dates for wars and conflicts. We have bridges, tunnels, and streets named after October 6th for when the Sinai was won back from Israel. It sounds to us as natural to us as inserting freeway names, like saying 'the 405.'" For example, even without the year, #Jan25 is recognizable to users of social media as a signifier of the Tahrir demonstrations, because it functions as an #Event hashtag.

To understand how hashtags could be archived, grouped, and visualized, Sakr led the technical team that created R-Shief, a research tool designed to interpret global digital social movements. Some of her most interesting visualizations show messages with two place-names referenced that are made proximate to each other even if they are from different parts of the world. For example, a visualization that analyzes the #Ferguson data set with a #Gaza filter shows a distinct pattern of zigzagging bands that move across a blue to green to magenta spectrum. Using metadata harvested from millions of tweets, Sakr sees "a lot of people bringing these two seemingly unrelated things together."

#NOISE

Hope Jahren might seem to be an unlikely attacker. As a mild-mannered scientist, she probably doesn't see herself as a person who did any serious harm. Chances are she believes she only helped a misguided hashtag find its true purpose. Nonetheless, there are people who perceive her "hashtag hijacking" activities as vandalism at the very least, if not a threat to their livelihoods or an assault on a peaceful community undeserving of her aggressive intentions.

Jahren doesn't talk about hashtag hijacking in her 2016 memoir *Lab Girl*. This book tells not only Jahren's own life story as a geobiologist but also the life stories of the seeds, roots, leaves, and flowers that she analyzes as a botanist and geochemist studying the isotopes of photosynthesis. Personal disclosures in her autobiography include admitting doubts during her pregnancy about motherhood, revealing the precarity of her laboratory's finances, and confessing her deep emotional attachment to her chief lab assistant Bill Hagopian. She also chronicles battles with mental illness, which were so severe that without medication she would bang her head until bloody and bruised. The most bizarre scene in the book conveys the anguish of her struggles with bipolar disorder when Jahren describes coming to her senses after a bout of mania to find one of her teeth—mingled with her blood, mucus, and hair—on the floor.

In the narrative of *Lab Girl* Jahren compares her teenage vision of herself sitting on a stool at a laboratory workstation "picking out exactly the right little bottles of concentrated drugs" to the activities of "a rich woman" who "confidently seizes upon the perfect shade of nail polish before her manicure."[1] Of course, being a "lab girl" required renouncing any shiny surface areas subject to contamination, so the nicety of polished nails had to be abandoned in favor of what Jahren calls a "frazzled 'natural' look."

In 2013 Jahren gained notoriety for "hashtag hijacking" #ManicureMonday, a tag established for grooming-conscious readers of *Seventeen* magazine. Jahren posted a photo of her fingers smudged with blue highlighter with the #ManicureMonday label. Soon other female scientists were posting pictures of their hands being busy in a variety of scientific workplaces. #ManicureMonday photos showed professional women holding live animal specimens, measuring the size of feces, assembling ancient clay artifacts, shutting down telescopes, and operating centrifuges. Sometimes their nails were obscured by rubber gloves or protective gear. Using the hashtag for the better part of a year, Jahren posted photos of herself digging into buckets of soil, sorting cuttings, measuring lab plants, and performing other routine duties, which she also described in the unhashtagged prose of *Lab Girl*.

The term "hashtag hijacking" had already been in use for at least a year and was often deployed to describe how disgruntled customers might disrupt a corporate Twitter campaign. For example, in 2012 the hashtag for #McDStories was hijacked by fast-food patrons eager to share horror stories about the chain. Prior to Jahren's stunt the hashtags of drugstore retailers (#ILoveWalgreens), grocery stores (#WaitroseReasons), and airlines (#QuantasLuxury) had also been hijacked—often with photos shaming corporate brands for shoddy service.

Hashtag hijacking can do real social violence to the initial participants. After the shooting of Michael Brown by a Ferguson police officer, when news organizations posted "thuggish" pictures of the dead man rather than photos of him as a student and family member, hashtag activists created #IfTheyGunnedMeDown to post dual photos of themselves that contrasted what media outlets would choose to reinforce anti-black stereotypes and what they would choose as representative of their aspirations and achievements. For example, @DevGriffin618 juxtaposed a picture of himself flashing hand signs and one in his graduation cap and gown.

At one point white supremacists overwhelmed the #IfTheyGunnedMeDown stream with racist images of Harambe, a zoo gorilla that had been shot after a child fell into its pen, which had become a right-wing meme. Black activists reasserted some control over #IfTheyGunnedMeDown, but for months "top" choices returned by the Twitter algorithm continued to heavily favor content tagged by white teenagers and a number of joke memes.

Jahren used the "hijacking" term unapologetically in interviews. Using a popular hashtag designed to appeal to 700,000 *Seventeen* subscribers seemed like an effective way to interest young women in careers in science, as well as a visually catchy way to challenge gender norms. But not everyone was enthusiastic about her assumption that beauty culture was a vacuous pursuit. "Some women found it offensive," Jahren admitted. "They said we were somehow pushing yet another image of what they should be onto a place they had claimed for their art."[2]

Indeed, many original users felt that the postings of the interlopers on #ManicureMonday were highly inappropriate. Communications professor Michele White has written about Jahren's hijacking and has argued that the privileged scientists conveyed disrespect for expertise in nail art and contemptuously disregarded the labor around metadata that #ManicureMonday represented for its community. According to White, the women had worked hard to "create a supportive culture" to "expand their social capital." Furthermore, as White observes, before the scientists took over the hashtag, the nail art postings featured "a wide variety of skin tones" that demonstrated "the racial diversity of #ManicureMonday producers" in its first incarnation.[3] In contrast the hands of the female scientists using the hashtag in response to Jahren's exhortation almost entirely belonged to white women.

As a scientist Jahren should have shown more appreciation for the women's craftwork, given that skilled and precise manual labor is essential to the scientific enterprise. Nobody wants a multimillion-dollar experiment ruined by a clumsy or careless neophyte under the delusion that science is primarily a mental activity and that dexterity doesn't matter.

From a life in science Jahren also knew the importance of the naming conventions that make scientific discourse possible. Being allowed to name something was an honor often associated with its discovery. Even with thousands of unnamed species and constant flux in applying and removing appellations, the investments made in coining a term and the deliberative processes behind every label were generally respected. Of course, naming a planet to memorialize a deceased pet or to promote a home business was strongly discouraged. But in comparison to the elaborate rules for astronomical bodies, the guidelines for naming species in the biological sciences were relatively broad. In short, the name must be spelled in the twenty-six characters of the Latin alphabet and must not be offensive. A completely arbitrary combination of letters was perfectly acceptable, and humorous names were not discouraged very rigorously as long as the rationale for choosing a particular term was defensible. For example, species have been named after movie characters from *Harry Potter* and *Star Wars*.[4]

The longevity of a hijacking attempt can be platform-dependent. Today there are no traces of Jahren's hijacking on Instagram. One can scroll through hundreds of

#ManicureMonday photos and see nothing but the work of nail art enthusiasts. From fluorescent claws to glittering jellybeans, there seem to be no remaining signs of Jahren's activist agenda. In contrast, the Twitter platform is still contested territory between opposing camps using the same hashtag. #ManicureMonday has photos showing jewel-like bottles of polish and lavish spa treatments, and it also has posts about second wave feminism and paleontology using the tag.

#CHATTER

Eunsong Kim's Twitter handle, @clepsydras, makes an arcane reference to an ancient time-measuring mechanism. In Classical Greece the clepsydra measured speeches in the law courts using the flow of water, much like an hourglass uses the flow of sand. The device consisted of two vessels, one placed at a higher level and filled with water. The speaker could continue speaking until the vessel at the lower level was full. The word comes from the same Greek root as "kleptomaniac," "to steal," because the water is stolen from its source.

One can see a terracotta example of a clepsydra from the fifth century BCE at the Agora Museum in Athens, which houses artifacts excavated from this early forum for commerce and democracy. This specimen bears the remains of two inscriptions: "ANTIO," meaning it was the property of the Antiochis tribe, and "XX" indicating the vessel's capacity of 6.4 liters. The water-clock on display took about six minutes to empty.

Today these very short speeches are called "lightning talks," and they vary from five minutes (Ignite style) to six minutes and forty seconds (PechaKucha style). @clepsydras is a clever name to choose for Twitter, because its microblogging platform was similarly optimized for brevity, limiting every user to extremely brief 140-character messages. (In 2017 the number was raised to a still-condensed 280.)

The clepsydra could also be used as a communication device in its own right. As a form of ancient telegraphy, two people sharing information could acquire a matched set of these clay pots and then inscribe the same messages at each horizontal level of the interior. At the first smoke signal both the sender of the message and the receiver allowed water to fall from their cylinders at a uniform rate. When the sender's gauge had reached the desired line, the sender sent a second smoke signal to the recipient who stopped the water flow and noted the equivalent line on the apparatus.

Like twins speaking the same secret language, this antiquated system relied on an idiosyncratically coded private circuit of communication. But in many ways its structure of data and metadata reflects our own age of electronic communication. The messages on the interior of the pots were the data; the smoke signals were the metadata.

In her offline life, @clepsydras/Kim is an English professor, poet, art educator, and activist who joined the #CancelColbert campaign after the movement's founder Suey Park operationalized the hashtag. Park had become incensed when a @ColbertReport account seemingly associated with the satiric award-winning television show known for poking fun at conservatives, tweeted what appeared to be a bizarre racist message at 4:02PM, on March 27, 2014: "I am willing to show #Asian community I care by introducing the Ching Chong Ding-Dong Foundation for Sensitivity to Orientals or Whatever."

The @ColbertReport message echoed old racist taunts mocking the supposed sound of the Chinese language. In John Steinbeck's *Cannery Row* one version of the rhyme is recorded for posterity: "Ching Chong, Chinaman sitting on a rail—'Long came a white man an' chopped off his tail."[1] This doggerel gained a new life in a 2014 viral video created by UCLA student Alexandra Wallace who mimicked what she considered to be the speech of international students as "ching chong ling long ting tong."

There were other offensive aspects to the @ColbertReport post. Using "Asian" as a catch-all term seemed to ignore complex national, ethnic, linguistic, and religious histories that differentiated China from its geographical neighbors. Dropping the expected article "the" before #Asian perpetuated stereotypes about immigrants' faulty English. Furthermore, the word "Oriental," which was associated with centuries of colonialism and exploitation by the Occident, represented a word choice widely seen as derogatory. Concluding the message with "Whatever," which expressed disregard for careful attention to avoiding offense, would have been recognized by many Internet users as a rhetorical move known to incite online flame wars.

Park was eating dinner when she saw the @ColbertReport message. Using her "Angry Asian Woman" account, @suey_ park, which has since been scraped of all content, she posted the following reply: "The Ching Chong Ding-Dong Foundation for Sensitivity to Orientals has decided to call for #CancelColbert. Trend it." The hashtag was soon trending as Park had commanded. It became highly visible for many on the main navigation bar of Twitter's site. The hashtag had been picked up by Park's followers and then by their followers within Park's orbit of extremely active online community members devoted to calling out racism against Asian Americans.

There were also a number of additional accelerants that caused #CancelColbert to trend quickly. The social network of participants had a shared sense of purpose and was committed to maintaining the infrastructures that defined their existence. The slogan was a clear call to action that used a familiar formula, the consumer boycott. Hashtags calling for shunning a particular organization could be extremely potent for corporations (#DeleteUber) and even cultural institutions (#DontDoDartmouth). Additionally, alliterative hashtags are especially appealing as mnemonic devices. Event planners counseling engaged couples about choosing hashtags tend to recommend alliterative hashtags like #WilsonWedding or #MorrisonMarriage for easier recall.

As a media critic Park already had a successful track record of creating viral hashtag slogans that had similarly challenged the Eurocentrism of other popular television shows. Park's #HowIMetYourRacism hashtag publicized the insensitivity of a kung fu tribute episode of the popular situation comedy

How I Met Your Mother in which white characters appeared in "yellowface" as exotic Asian caricatures.

Within days #CancelColbert stories appeared in the *New Yorker*, the *Nation*, *Salon*, *USA Today*, and other prominent publications. Meanwhile the *Colbert Report* television show was distancing itself from the offensive tweet, and the tweeter was distancing the tweet from the television show. Apparently the @ColbertReport account was not affiliated with the production company. It has since been deleted from Twitter. The officially sanctioned @StephenAtHome account attempted to use humor to defuse the conflict with Park and her critics: "#CancelColbert—I agree! Just saw @ColbertReport tweet. I share your rage. Who is that, though? I'm @StephenAtHome." A few days later, in addressing the #CancelColbert controversy directly on the late-night show, the comedy host summarized events in a way that reduced them to a simple misunderstanding blown out of proportion:

> To recap, a web editor I've never met posted a tweet in my name on an account I don't control, outrages a hashtag activist, and the news media gets seventy-two hours of content. The system worked. But all this started right after I taped Thursday night's show, so I couldn't respond until Monday. So in in a sense, I was canceled—for three days.

However, Park's objections were not completely ungrounded. The offensive tweet was based on a line from the actual show in which Colbert's fictional right-wing persona ridiculed outrage over the name of an American football team, the Washington Redskins, by comparing the designation to a fictional Asian "mascot" named "Ching Chong." Ching Chong was supposedly on the show's letterhead and received awards as a surrogate for the show's host.

The writers of the satiric dialogue that Colbert spoke obviously agreed that the term "redskin" denigrated distinct nations of indigenous peoples with a blanket racial slur. The segment focused on the fact that the Redskins' owner Daniel Snyder had begun a nonprofit foundation to benefit native tribes in a bid to improve bad public relations with Indian groups. By naming the organization the "Washington Redskins Original Americans Foundation" Snyder only made matters worse. Yet *The Colbert Report*'s decision to show the outrageousness of the "Redskins" name by comparing it to "Ching Chong Ding Dong" taunts was unacceptable to Park, who argued that white liberals would never broadcast racial slurs about Jews or African Americans. Furthermore, in the original segment Colbert mimics a foreign accent, cites an invented "Asian Media Watch" group, makes jokes about opium pipes and rickshaws, and announces the formation of the "Ching Chong Ding-Dong Foundation for Sensitivity to Orientals or Whatever."

Park was subjected to vitriolic racism and misogyny online as she gained more national visibility for #CancelColbert. On Twitter those who ridiculed her added racist hashtags like #MeLoveYouLongTime and #CHINGCHONGDINGDONG to the #CancelColbert hashtag. Although "Suey" was a pseudonym, Park's antagonists seized on her real identity. Menacing cyberstalkers added blueprints of Park's house, death records, and other threatening hints that they intended to do her harm. Private information, including her personal phone number and confidential information on college transcripts, was widely circulated thanks to a malevolent Reddit group.

In a 2018 interview Kim described trying to help Park cope with the onslaught of publicity. As a precarious freelance writer and former graduate student, Park had few resources to draw upon for aid. Kim was also in a relatively powerless position as a teaching assistant in graduate school at the University of California, San Diego, but she found her academic training helpful for coordinating a plan.

Kim laughed about the irony of doing "what grad school prepares you for," as she worked on statements with Park and wrote reading responses to demonstrate that those behind #CancelColbert were capable of more nuanced thinking. Showing argumentative complexity when the campaign's inventors were being characterized as overly sensitive, one-dimensional, and humorless would be key to regaining control of the hashtag and the larger cultural conversation that had begun spinning out of control.

Many of the #CancelColbert tweets that attempted to overthrow the premises of the original conversation called for other popular television shows to be cancelled on the grounds of faux political correctness. These hashtags included #CancelSupernatural, #CancelTheBigBangTheory, and #CancelMikeAndMolly. Others like #CancelTheFirst Amendment sarcastically suggested barring free speech entirely. Many others, such as #CancelAsianTwitter, expressed a desire to nullify the social media presence of Asian voices entirely.

Because of the deluge of tens of thousands of messages on Twitter with the #CancelColbert hashtag, rather than rebut tweets individually, Park and Kim focused on major news organizations to get their messages across. In an opinion piece published on the website for *Time* magazine the two women stated their convictions firmly:

> The entertainment industry has perfected the development of white, cis, straight, male characters. The marginalization of "other voices"—except when those "others" are brought in only to aid in the cheap punch line of a joke—is complete. This is aggression that we do not have to accept. We will protest this until it ends.[2]

In their *Time* manifesto Park and Kim also answered critics of their original response who identified as Asian American by asking if they were clamoring for the "honorary whiteness" bestowed upon a "model minority" who agrees to observe "codes of conduct" that protect the status quo.

Many of the consequences of visibility facilitated by the hashtag's success proved to be disastrous for Park. More and more people violently opposed to the anti-racist goals of the original campaign joined in #CancelColbert activities and intensified the white supremacist and misogynistic harassment that had blossomed soon after the tag trended. As the mood darkened, there were still occasional moments of levity and bravado among the original group. At one point Park, Kim, and other women of color on Twitter assumed male screen names and avatars. Suey Park became Stewy Park. The women watched scorn transform into adulation as they posted assertive messages that would have been dismissed contemptuously before. But personal threats terrorized Park and undermined her confidence that she would be allowed to assume any role as a public figure without becoming even more vulnerable to constant abuse. Personal relationships deteriorated under stress, and Park withdrew from social media and relocated geographically in her face-to-face world.

The debut of the 2016 television series *The Internet Ruined My Life* featured Park's traumatic encounters in her life after #CancelColbert. In the show Park explained that she didn't actually wish for the *Colbert* show to be taken off the air, but she did want something "catchy and over-the-top to get my point across." The opening shots of the episode depict a creepy reenactment of being taunted by a figure outside her window. In a scene straight out of a horror movie the stalker insinuates that Park is in his gun sights and reveals that he knows she is wearing a red pajama top. Later he identifies himself as an "ex-military sniper" and warns her to "prepare to die." In the harrowing days and months that followed this incident, after experiencing the discouraging response of law enforcement and deciding to flee her home in favor of a life of safehouses and burner phones, Park found it difficult to rebuild the life that she had once enjoyed.

Kim was fortunate to be spared the worst aspects of #CancelColbert, although she experienced some harassment as well. Moreover, as an academic, Kim was able to use the analytical methods of her training in critical theory to intellectually process the implications of what she calls the "visibility and unexpected visualization" that hashtags make possible. In reflecting on how the media reported on results generated by Twitter's algorithm, Kim has sought to expose how "privatized, opaque institutions of selective coverage are working with other privatized, opaque institutions of selective timelines to define what's public, what's universal, what's important."[3]

In other words, whenever a company like Twitter uses its platform to make something visible, like #CancelColbert, it also uses its platform to make other things invisible, like the original conversations that energized the network of Asian American digital content-creators. Furthermore, as the intimidation of Suey Kim demonstrates, visibility can be unwelcome when it is used a tool for designating people as outcasts, potential criminals, or targets of abuse.

Looking at the metadata management of companies like Twitter, which restrict how long a message can be shown as trending, Kim began to see something even more insidious. As she explained, "a 'trend' is based on a very specific definition of 'now' and 'new,' a definition that we as users do not have access to." Kim studied other campaigns of hashtag activism—such as #Ferguson, #FreePalestine, or #OccupyWallStreet—and why they might fail to show as trending topics. She saw that often the metrics that Twitter provided didn't make sense, especially when she compared them to hashtags that relatively few people were using with banal messages about birthdays or sports teams.

Although the algorithms that generate the most prominently listed results in the display of trending topics exist inside a black box of proprietary code owned by Twitter's corporate platform, with a little ingenuity and some technical knowledge users can independently create their own charts. But Kim cautioned that many "different kinds of analytic programs" capable of generating objective "real-time results" for tracking hashtag popularity and frequency, which had been available in the past, might not be available in the future. Topsy, the tool that Kim had used to show that official Twitter trending data was misleading, was bought by Apple for 200 million dollars and then shut down two years later. Kim described a pattern in which real-time analytic companies were either acquired or ceased to exist, perpetuating a lack of checks and balances on Twitter and other social media companies. Kim has argued that this is the equivalent of stock manipulation in a supposedly open marketplace of ideas.

As Kim points out, the ability to invent a hashtag and thus assign metadata to a specific set of related future conversations may give users of high-tech authoring platforms a false sense of confidence that they have agency and control. As the exercise of free speech becomes increasingly dependent upon powerful technology companies with potential monopolies, possible solutions to problems in platform governance become increasingly difficult for legislators and technologists to solve. After all, these companies' business models extract profit from offering supposedly free content via targeted advertising and the sale of user data that depends upon intimate knowledge of users' personal preferences, emotional sentiments, and social relations that had previously been unmonetized.

Prior media technologies in the so-called culture industry that were criticized by Marxist German intellectuals for hawking fantasies and fetishes were relatively straightforward by comparison. Attempts at media manipulation with subliminal advertising or behavioral conditioning in the analog era always had to contend with free presses and independent media that could control the means of production. In contrast, networked communication depends on shared protocols that are impossible to resist. Metadata can be contributed by users at the proper points of attachment following all of the rules and still be effectively filtered out or discarded if it is in the company's financial interest to amplify other metadata that is more lucrative. Nonetheless, users continue in good faith to assume that appending metadata to other media content is now part of the circuit of reception.

Eunsong Kim is also well aware of the problem of white privilege dominating the larger conversation about digital rights and wrongs. In an essay written collaboratively with Dorothy Kim called "The #TwitterEthics Manifesto" she excoriates academics, reporters, and other public intellectuals who claim to speak for digital communities of color that are perfectly capable of speaking for themselves. They note that token attention gets paid when there is online harassment or cyberstalking of people of color, but activities like quoting out of context and without permission, scraping data without consent of the people in the conversation, and profiting off the digital labor of others are frequently rewarded in support of the ideologies of white liberalism.[4]

By this point in the book readers may have noticed that most of my experts on hashtag use—the ones whose voices I include from interviews—are women and that many are women of color. This is a deliberate choice to make Kim, Patheja, Abidin, Sakr, and other women of color prominent in telling the story of the hashtag. This book also undoubtedly has its blind spots. As a treatise on the hashtag, it inevitably reflects my own bourgeois upbringing and my personal freedom from precarity. As much as I have traveled around the world researching its subject matter, it is likely biased in certain respects. Of course, taking a comprehensive view is challenging when the task is so ambitious. The hashtag is a cultural artifact with a long double helix of interrelated design history—one strand composed of human-to-human communication and one strand composed of machine-to-machine discourse—and the white male engineers and programmers at Bell Labs and Twitter cannot be completely ignored.

Eunsong Kim urges us to see hashtags as inextricably linked to long histories of oppression and liberation and to consider who has access to the public sphere and under what conditions. Kim writes that "hashtags are digitalized fragments of political ancestry; ongoing, replenished, connected to and beyond their current framework." According to this way of thinking metadata isn't simply an external appendage that provides a handy label or convenient signpost to the substrate of our political realities. Metadata *is* the substrate, much like pieces of genetic material that are constantly colliding and mutating, and it produces our political realities.

#FILE

The world can be divided into two types of people: those who are enamored of file folders and those who are not.

Having worked my entire adult life for the government—first at a youth services agency and then for a series of state-run universities—I believe that the file folder should be the primary unit of any organization. After all, the word "bureaucracy" etymologically refers to the desks and offices in which paperwork was filed away—in shelves, pigeonholes, and drawers before the invention of the file folder. In his classic work on bureaucracy, Max Weber claimed that the maintenance of files was central to institutional memory.[1]

My husband is of the opposite philosophy. Although my computer desktop is neatly organized with folders that progress reasonably from "Articles" to "William and Mary," his desktop is a tangle of cluttered icons and superimposed words.

For him, the physical file folder is an object to be mocked and vandalized. It is material to be cut up for cardboard. One year he took all of our folders that held important family papers and replaced all the tabs with rebuses. The file for "grants" had a picture of the cigar-chomping Civil War general Ulysses S. Grant instead of words. Many of the rebuses were elaborate. Some had multiple pictures and plus or minus signs to create the appropriate letter combinations. This scheme made alphabetization extremely cumbersome.

This resistance to the violence of alphabetization has its logic. The ordering of surnames perpetuates many injustices. If you are earlier in the alphabet, your lateness is more likely to be noticed in a roll call. If you are later in the alphabet, you are less likely to receive credit on publications. Because the alphabet is an arbitrary construction, the preservation of culture can depend on happenstance. During his lifetime the ancient Greek dramatist Euripides wrote almost a hundred plays, but many of the nineteen that survive today only were conserved by freak accident. One volume from Euripides' massive collected works labeled eta through kappa—E–K—remained undisturbed for centuries in a monastic collection.

In imagining virtual file folders, companies who manufacture accounting software struggle with the basic metadata problem of sensible labeling. When profit and loss statements need to be demarcated into separate categories within the larger obvious binary of "income" and "expenses," sorting transactions can be difficult. Does "painting" belong in the category of "maintenance," "repair," or "improvements"? Each word has different implications for how an asset is evaluated and even taxed.

But in the digital world it seems that things can also go in more than one folder. For example, in the bins of a traditional record shop of the past with conventional divisions between genres like "folk" or "punk," albums could only occupy one physical section in the store. But now that digital items in online stores can be labeled with multiple attributes and be located algorithmically through variable search paths, the same album can not only be categorized as both "folk" and "punk," but can be also described as "alternative" music, "indy rock," and even "indie rock." Similarly, thanks to new digital dropboxes, the same document can live in more than one digital folder simultaneously.

Some argue that this general shift from filing to tagging in applying metadata labels will make decision-making about categories less arduous since no one will be forced to choose between options. In *Everything Is Miscellaneous* David Weinberger celebrates what he calls "the new digital disorder" in which computerization makes multiple schemes for categorical possibilities much less difficult.[2] Rather than rely on file folders, decision charts, and organizational trees, Weinberger claims that modern metadata will allow businesses and governments to find resources easily that would otherwise be hidden by the rationality of exclusion.

Unfortunately humans can be terrible categorizers of shared metadata. In a 2007 conference paper, Hend Al-Khalifa and Hugh Davis studied tagging patterns on the social bookmarking site Del.icio.us.[3] During its heyday in the mid-2000s—before social media platforms came to dominate Internet use—Del.icio.us was a popular service for keeping track of useful websites and sharing popular pages with others.

After categorizing over ten thousand tags on the service, the authors concluded that 34 percent of the labels on Del.icio.us only served personal utility. Such labels might read "toHugh," "myBlog," "toRead," etc. With user-generated tagging on Del.icio.us, only a measly 5 percent of tags were clearly useful to others. Terms like "Kool" and "Kickass" that would be anathema to fastidious librarians were common descriptors in these self-referential systems of tagging. My favorite Del.icio.us tag in their study had to be the self-evident "SaveThis."

Despite people's everyday incompetence, many fields are increasingly likely to require mastery of file-naming conventions in judging job performance. For example, artists creating special effects for movies can be fired for mislabeling a digital file. Often those in new digital professions must learn from the wisdom of librarians and archivists who are professionally trained in applying the rules of various classification systems to tag materials with metadata, whether they are working with collections of Dewey Decimal books in a small town local library or the massive RAMEAU system in the skyscrapers at the Bibliothèque nationale de France.

No matter what system they use, librarians know that classification can be extremely political. For example, outside agitators often challenge Library of Congress Subject Headings used in the United States. In 1971 Sanford Berman complained about the continuing existence of the "Jewish Question" subject heading, despite its historical ties to anti-Semitic thinking that had answered the question with a genocide.[4] The heading was finally removed in the spring of 1984. Thanks to the intervention of Filipino activists who rightfully challenged the norms of American colonialism, "Philippines—History—Insurrection, 1896–1898" was changed to "Philippines—History—Revolution, 1896–1898" in the online catalog by 1998.

According to archivist Dorothy Berry, metadata often privileges categories of people's names, institutional authors, and geographical locations rather than represents the discourses of social movements on their own terms.

> An example I often use to illustrate this issue is a record titled "Justice Department Report on the Shooting of Michael Brown by Ferguson, Missouri Police Officer Darren Wilson." The humanly defined set marked this record as relevant, but the computing system did not. When I share this example people react in shock—of course this record is relevant to African American history! The metadata for the file, however, included only the keywords "Civil Unrest," "Justice Department," "Michael Brown," "Darren Wilson," "Ferguson, Missouri." Those keywords meld together in the zeitgeist creating a shared set extended keywords like "Police Violence," and "Black Lives Matter," but the computer systems work only with the technical metadata tied to a record, not the intellectual metadata tied to contemporary understandings.[5]

In other words, our existing structures for archiving collections tend to make little room for how language functions dynamically in speech acts that expand our common understanding. As metadata becomes increasingly automated, such as when indexers work with pre-set drop-down menus with autosuggest functions, the advantages of access to a controlled vocabulary for naming conventions may be offset by its conservative biases.

Geoffrey Bowker and his late partner Susan Leigh Star wrote a treatise about classification and its unintended consequences called *Sorting Things Out*. This 1999 classic is still consulted for understanding why people struggle at performing such an essential task.[6] Star trained as a sociologist, and Bowker earned his PhD in the history and philosophy of science. His resumé also included a stint as a file clerk in the Australian archives. Together they examined what they called "information infrastructures" around the world to understand how categorization could have profound sociocultural effects.

Some of Bowker and Star's most important work was on racial classification in South Africa under the old twentieth-century apartheid regime that separated people geographically and politically based on skin color. People of native African descent were forced to live in tribal homelands or marginalized shantytowns while the descendants of white colonizers occupied the privileged centers of modern metropolises. The categories on identification cards determined where one was allowed to sleep at night. Bowker and Star examined how citizens of mixed heritage vexed the presumptions of what was supposed to be an orderly system. People might also try to get themselves reclassified with a less desirable status in the racial hierarchy in order to be allowed to live with their loved ones, if they had parents, partners, or children who were designated as belonging to a less prestigious race.

The Nazi racial state had similarly assumed clear boundaries between included and excluded populations. Using racial science Nazi experts were dumbfounded to find no basis for their belief in the firm separation between "Jewish blood" and "Aryan blood" upon which laws for "German blood" and "German honor" depended. Studying blood types with combinations of standard antigens and antibodies like O positive or B negative produced no clear patterns to distinguish Jews from non-Jews biologically. As a result German soldiers in World War II were denied what could have been life-saving blood transfusions and forced to take chances with less fortifying plasma that was assumed more racially pure. In the death camps, genocidal administrators used a seemingly innocuous term from the mail service *Sonderbehandlung*—"special handling"—to designate the prisoners who would be sent to the gas chambers.

Jessica Marie Johnson asks her fellow historians to look at the top row of the registers of enslaved persons and inquire about the work of categorization that has yet to be undone. Atop the 1841 ship's manifest of the brig *Orleans*, which was bound for Richmond, Virginia, the captives are labeled with "names," "sex," "age," "stature," "complexion," "shipper's name" (and "residence"), and "owner's or consignee's name" (and "residence"). No other information about their identities appears worth recording, even though one of the people below decks, Solomon Northup, had been born free and had maintained a successful musical career before being abducted from what was supposed to be a fiddle performance for a traveling circus.

Johnson wants us to understand that metadata is not separable from data. Metadata is not like a barnacle that attaches itself to ship; it is like an organism that interacts with another dynamic entity. The data that we collect is shaped by our existing organizational strategies, just as the columns of a spreadsheet anticipate particular kinds of information.

There are alternatives to systems of categorization that enforce rigid divisions. Star also looked at how bird fanciers divided specimens into types. Working with James Griesemer she studied how professional ornithologists differed from amateurs in sorting out species of birds.[7] Their site of analysis—The Museum of Vertebrate Zoology at the University of California, Berkeley—was founded as an establishment of scientific research in the early twentieth century and was thus quite unlike other natural history institutions that evolved from idiosyncratically displayed cabinets of curiosities. At the museum taxidermied bird specimens were frequently labeled and relabeled. Both trained scientists and birdwatchers from the lay public used the same stuffed collection. Star reasoned that even if different groups failed to reach consensus about how a bird should be classified, at least they were using the same collection of objects for the communal work of sense-making. Star called these shared taxonomic materials "boundary objects" and argued that they were more flexible and useful than the Linnaean classification system that assumed that everything could be divided into mutually exclusive nested boxes scaling down through Kingdom, Phylum, Class, Order, Family, Genus, and Species.

In examining the materiality of information infrastructures, media historian Shannon Mattern has looked at the long history of metadata and how it is inextricably linked to physical objects of architecture and interior design. From the time that scrolls were positioned on shelves to the advent of clear plastic tabs for hanging folders in cabinets, metadata and furniture have been interdependent systems.

Some name Callimachus as the first large-scale metadata maker in the ancient world. About 245 BCE this Libyan of Greek parentage was entrusted with undertaking a grand bibliographic survey of all the contents of the Library of Alexandria, essentially the first library catalog. The task of inventorying almost a half a million papyrus scrolls was daunting and produced a collection of descriptions that was supposedly 120 volumes itself. His task was probably made easier by a predecessor, Zenodotus, who had already placed the scrolls in order and affixed identifying tags with author, title, and subject.

Of course, as a human instinct, the informational labels of metadata predate the classical age. Hieroglyphic inscriptions mark Egyptian funerary objects with labels. Some of the earliest written texts from Uruk in Mesopotamia list officials by name and by designation, such as leader of the city, leader of the law, leader of the plow, and leader of the lambs. It could be argued that metadata existed before written language, particularly if our human forebears treated decorative baskets, barrels, boxes, or vases as sorting mechanisms.

In other words, metadata has traditionally had a connection to the physical objects of the material world, whether they be wooden furniture or stuffed bird corpses. However, media theorist Katherine Hayles observes that information "lost its body" after post-World War II cyberneticists substituted an abstracted pattern of signifiers that could be translated to any medium.[8] According to Hayles, a sequence of ones and zeros in a digital file could represent any kind of sensory experience—sight, sound, touch, and even smell. With so many heterogeneous digital files buzzing between billions of locations, metadata becomes even more essential as a finding aid.

#METADATA

Wendy America Hester was probably the first person to cause me to think seriously about metadata. She was a friend in graduate school. Her dissertation was about collectors. She wrote about the library that Frankfurt School cultural critic Walter Benjamin had cherished and about how the difficulties of its transportation had fatally delayed his escape from the German authorities. She also wrote about the artist Joseph Cornell, who created elaborate boxes with assemblages of found objects. She was a polymath who spoke several languages fluently but struggled to find a home in academia.

After we left graduate school she worked in the film industry as a set decorator. She managed inventories of props and continuity lists. Her mind had a sharp facility with organizing complex collections of items that was useful in many contexts. At the same time she had horrible migraine headaches and was depressed. She took her own life just after she turned forty.

She told me she wasn't born Wendy America Hester. She said she added the "America" because she thought it improved the sound of her name. It amused her that people assumed her parents were hippies or hyper-patriots as a result. It was metadata included in her obituary.

Before graduate school Wendy had worked at the photo archive of the *New York Times*, where she labeled photographs and sorted them into folders and drawers. It could be tedious work in the newspaper's "morgue," she admitted, but she said it was also surprisingly intellectually challenging. If the photographer had a signed release from the subject depicted in the image or that person was a notable figure, the task could be simplified. For example, Wendy took home duplicate photographs of Jean-Paul Sartre and Simone de Beauvoir as souvenirs. But many of the images in the newspaper file drawers didn't illustrate the lives of famous people. They showed celebrations and conflicts of various kinds at various scales. They displayed inanimate objects that might be best described with foreign vocabularies. They included editorial images—which could not be re-used for advertising or promotions—and stock images that were purchased with licensing fees.

Photojournalists today are much less likely to have permanent positions with newspapers like the *New York Times*. Consequently metadata has become even more important to the profession of image-making. The ownership of digital images, the information they depict, and the context of production can be hotly contested, whether it involves disputes about intellectual property or accusations of fake news.

In 2016 I attended the preview of a new software platform at the International Center of Photography. It was named Four Corners after its interface design. Tapping each of the image's right angle points would allow users to see more information about the picture. The lower left corner of the photograph would contain the back-story of the scene with data "provided by the photographer, the subject, a witness or other sources." The upper left corner would contain additional image documentation "where photographs made before and after, a video of the scene or a comparative image could be presented." The upper right corner would have links to "online articles, videos, maps and other information." The bottom right corner would be where the reader could find "the caption, credit, copyright (or Creative Commons license), and a code of ethics."

Four Corners asserted the presence of three stakeholders in every image: the photographer, the subject, and the audience. By offering a richer range of metadata than the content labels that might be conventionally attached to an image, the platform aspired to enable the photographer "to frame the issue" and "the audience to engage directly with the issues and connect to the protagonists at the very moment they are most moved."[1] In this way the metadata might reflect the will of more participants in the larger media ecology in which the image was produced and consumed.

In demos Four Corners used the famed *Saigon Execution* photo of Eddie Adams, which shows the 1968 shooting of a supposed Viet Cong operative in what was then the capital of

South Vietnam. The killing of Nguyễn Văn Lém was carried out personally by the national Chief of Police Nguyễn Ngọc Loan. Adams won the Pulitzer Prize for this photograph, which captures the exact moment of the man's impending death with a weapon pointed at his temple. The *Washington Post* marveled that in "1/500th of a second, Adams caught the moment the bullet crashed through the Viet Cong prisoner's skull at about 600 mph, distorting his face, tousling his hair and shoving his head off center."[2] It belongs to a genre of images that Susan Sontag has described as "among the most celebrated and often reproduced of war photographs," which expresses the "mystery" and "indecency" of co-spectatorship at the precise instant of the expiration of a unique human life.[3]

Time magazine justified the murder by describing the victim "as the captain of a terrorist squad who had just killed the family of one of Loan's friends,"[4] and Adams defended the gunman's righteousness in interviews and documentaries about his career. But the callousness of dispensing with judge and jury and the suffering of the grimacing man with his hands behind his back became a symbol for the violence and arbitrariness of the entire Vietnam War. Adams's inability to control the interpretation of his image was a source of deep frustration up until the end of his life in 2004. If Adams could have maintained his grip on the image by indelibly attaching metadata to *Saigon Execution*, he would have likely instructed the viewer to read the image as he did.

Elements of the Adams photograph were replicated for many different purposes. Some were completely divorced from the original context of the work of photojournalism or the role of a war correspondent. Since Adams pressed the shutter *Saigon Execution* has appeared in anti-war posters, T-shirts, street art, a Woody Allen film, a tableau of LEGO toys, a print by a Brazilian artist created from memory, and hundreds of Internet memes.

Contemporary digital cameras often automatically generate metadata, inextricably binding it up with the alphanumerical code of the image itself. Today's mobile devices can interweave time, location, IP address, and type of device into the digital file. This traceability can create complications for human rights groups that desire to document abuses by authoritarian regimes with conclusive evidence of wrongdoing—and counter incidents of fake photos—but do not want to compromise the identities of vulnerable witnesses and whistleblowers. WITNESS, a nonprofit organization based in New York City, is developing applications like ObscuraCam, which strips out metadata and blurs faces, and InformaCam, which improves the reliability of metadata if the photographer wants to record definitive proof that cannot be dismissed as a forgery.

This book has focused on the deliberative processes that human beings participate in to reach consensus about naming conventions. However, futurists predict that most tasks of classification will inevitably be transferred to machines. Hashtag use has accelerated this process of automation, as large social network sites with millions of images use the metadata supplied by users to train machine learning systems, so that they can identify untagged images as well. These intelligent systems learn not only from the humans who author hashtags, but also from the humans who search for specific hashtags on search engines and social network platforms.

Applications like Photerloo can add appealing hashtags to an image of the Northern Lights such as #OutdoorFun or #SkyPorn automatically. I uploaded an official faculty photo of myself, and the algorithm generated factual hashtags like #Woman, #Glasses, and #Outdoors. Then it suggested more effervescent hashtags to increase the probability of online buzz like #Girlz, #Suited, and #PeopleWhoDoFunStuff in translating my image to metadata text.

With so-called custom emojis automatically inserting a miniature digital picture to stand in for particular hashtags, the reverse translation from text to image can also be automated. For example, using a hashtag about viewing the 2016 U.S. presidential debates might automatically suggest substitution of a small podium. The hashtag for being a fan of a particular K-pop boy band in 2018 may produce a tiny bulletproof vest. This book has considered the impact of "hashtag revolutions" on civic life, but perhaps it should also reflect on the potential consequences of the "emoji revolutions" to come.

The use of artificial intelligence even makes it possible for machines to author the characters that compose a new hashtag based on prior patterns of word combination popularity, much as computer programs can independently write sonnets or screenplays using algorithms. Yet the more that our digital culture becomes automated, the more human it becomes, because new machine learning technologies depend on the organic labor of living teachers and curators who must establish the parameters of training sets and design the simple childlike initial tasks that make sophisticated artificial intelligence possible.

In our present moment that gives primacy to metadata in an era of information excess we can see that the long history of the evolution of conventions for human-to-human communication and those of machine-to-machine communication have become increasingly intertwined. Rather than outsource the labor of naming to computational agents or denigrate these conventions as mindless, we need to become more conscious and intentional partners with the digital technologies that we depend upon.

The lessons learned from adept hashtag users can be applied to many situations in our increasingly hybridized discourses, as people use languages that have become inseparably human and machine. In many ways this is an information revolution with profound philosophical consequences that may be more radical than the advent of silent reading in the era of Saint Augustine. Calling out hashtags that are expected to be the unspoken parts of a message is a way to acknowledge the adoption of new practices that were once alien. Like silent reading, these practices also challenge previous expectations about privacy and publicity. When government agencies reassure the public that they are "only" collecting "metadata" rather than conducting full-scale surveillance, citizens should be skeptical. When technology companies control information about metadata statistics to rig popularity contests, users should challenge their claims to proprietary trade secrets.

By memorializing people, landmarking places, reciting slogans, promoting brands, and planning events with hashtags, political, social, and economic life is being conducted. Metadata has become how people communicate.

Marshall McLuhan insisted a half-century ago that "the medium is the message."[5]

Now the metadata is the message.

#ACKNOWLEDGMENTS

This book distills a decade of conversations about the hashtag as a cultural object with at least a hundred knowledgeable people. For their insights about civic media I am particularly grateful to Beth Coleman, Jennifer Cool, Joan Donovan, Henry Jenkins, Dorothy Kim, Nicholas Mirzoeff, Ramesh Srinivasan, and Jacqueline Wernimont for their essential contributions to this project. Ed Eckert, the current Bell Labs archivist, was consulted for #OCTOTHORPE. #PERSON was constructed from conversations with Jasmeen Patheja, Nishant Shah, Shobha SV, and Radhika Takru, as well as input from the faculty and students of Sarai. #PLACE was shaped by interviews and email exchanges with Maksym Dvorovy, Yevhen Fedchenko, Kateryna Kruk, Andrew Lytvyn, Vitaliy Moroz, Natalia Neshevets, and Olegsiy Radynski and the guidance of Tetyana Bohdanova, Lev Manovich, and Svitlana Matviyenko. #SLOGAN cites the work of Judith Butler, who is also my colleague on the Executive Council of the Modern Language Association. It also draws heavily on conversations with Moya Bailey and Mikki Kendall from the Center for Solutions to

Online Violence. #BRAND depends largely on an extensive interview with Crystal Abidin. Before encountering Abidin's work as a result of participation in the Selfie Course and the Selfies Researchers group, my understanding of the discourses of self-branding was developed by Ellen Lupton and Julia Lupton. Much of #INTERSECTION relied on an interview with Laila Shereen Sakr. Michele White's research was central to the argument of #NOISE, and the faculty reading group at William & Mary who discussed *Lab Girl* contributed to my perspective on Hope Jahren's career. I was fortunate to be able to draw on an interview with Eunsong Kim for #CHATTER. Ellen Strenski pointed me to the work of Max Weber for #FILE. Many thanks to Naomi Silver for her help with #METADATA and her expertise in digital rhetoric offered on the manuscript more generally. Information about metadata in digital photographs in this final chapter came from Sam Gregory and Jonathan Worth. Jonathan Alexander, Cheryl Ball, James J. Brown Jr., Doug Eyman, Andrea Lunsford, and Annette Vee offered models for scholarship in digital rhetoric and shaped directions in the field. Faculty and graduate students at the Equality Lab at William & Mary were also important participants in the writing process, particularly Jessica Cowing, Lindsay Garcia, Jennifer Ross, Ravynn Stringfield, and Khanh Vo. Funding from Dean Kate Conley at William and Mary, Bill Maurer from the Institute for Money, Technology, and Financial Inclusion at U.C. Irvine, and boards disbursing faculty research funds at U.C. San Diego were critical for undertaking field work in

India and Ukraine. The editors of the Object Lessons series, Ian Bogost and Christopher Schaberg, gave essential advice, and my fellow NEH Object Lesson workshop participants also provided invaluable feedback during the proposal development process. Of course these acknowledgments would be incomplete without an expression of sincerest thanks to Haaris Naqvi, Amy Martin, Katherine De Chant, Amy Jordan, Leeladevi Ulaganathan, David Campbell, and all of the Bloomsbury staff for bringing this project into print as one of these beautiful books.

NOTES

#Octothorpe

1 Fairbanks (Jerry) Productions, *Century 21 Calling*, 1964, http://archive.org/details/Century21964.

2 Mary Champion Lutz and Alphonse Chapanis, "Expected Locations of Digits and Letters on Ten-Button Keysets," *Journal of Applied Psychology* 39, no. 5 (1955): 314–17.

3 R. L. Deininger, "Human Factors Engineering Studies of the Design and Use of Pushbutton Telephone Sets," *Bell System Technical Journal* 39, no. 4 (July 1, 1960): 995–1012.

4 Doug Kerr, "The Pumpkin," The names "octatherp" and "octotherp" for the symbol "#," The Pumpkin, December 6, 2014, http://dougkerr.net/Pumpkin/index.htm#Octatherp_octotherp.

5 Keith Houston, *Shady Characters: The Secret Life of Punctuation, Symbols & Other Typographical Marks* (New York: Norton, 2014), 42.

6 Ernest Lawton Thurston, *Business Arithmetic for Secondary Schools* (New York: Macmillan, 1917), 419.

7 Ralph Carlsen, "Octothorpe (The Answer)," November 28, 1995, http://massis.lcs.mit.edu/telecom-archives/archives/history/octothorpe.the.real.story.

8   William Safire, "On Language; #@//( ) ! = Hash, At, Slash, Backslash, Open, Close, Bang," *The New York Times*, June 30, 1991, http://www.nytimes.com/1991/06/30/magazine/on-lang uage-hash-at-slash-backslash-open-close-bang.html.

#Inventor

1   Ian Yarett, "First Messages on Twitter, IM, Telegraph and More," *Newsweek*, September 7, 2009, http://www.newsweek. com/first-messages-twitter-im-telegraph-and-more-79479.

2   Jennifer Cool, "Speaking History to Technopower: An Ethnographic Account of the Making of Twitter" (Society for the Social Studies of Science, San Diego, CA, USA, October 11, 2013).

3   Dom Sagolla, *140 Characters: A Style Guide for the Short Form* (Hoboken, NJ: Wiley, 2009).

4   Christopher Kelty, "Geeks, Social Imaginaries, and Recursive Publics," *Cultural Anthropology* 20, no. 2 (May 1, 2005): 185–214, https://doi.org/10.1525/can.2005.20.2.185.

#Person

1   Elizabeth Losh, "Human Rights and Social Media in India: Blank Noise | DMLcentral," *DML Central: Digital Media and Learning* (blog), October 21, 2013, http://dmlcentral.net/blog/ liz-losh/human-rights-and-social-media-india-blank-noise.

2   "#SayHerName," AAPF, accessed May 24, 2018, http://www. aapf.org/sayhername/.

#Place

1 Manuel Castells, *Networks of Outrage and Hope: Social Movements in the Internet Age* (Malden, MA: Polity Press, 2015).

2 *Packingham v. North Carolina,* 2016, https://www.supremec ourt.gov/opinions/16pdf/15-1194_08l1.pdf.

3 "Internet Rights and Wrongs: Choices & Challenges in a Networked World," U.S. Department of State, accessed July 14, 2018, https://2009-2017.state.gov/secretary/20092013clinton/ rm/2011/02/156619.htm.

4 Vitaliy Moroz, *How Twitter Storm Works #digitalmaidan - Jan30 5.20 Pm Kyiv Time*, accessed May 23, 2018, https:// www.youtube.com/watch?v=hGZhh8oRzuw.

5 Zeynep Tufekci, "What Happens to #Ferguson Affects Ferguson:," *The Message* (blog), August 14, 2014, https://me dium.com/message/ferguson-is-also-a-net-neutrality-issue-6d2f3db51eb0.

6 "VK Blocks the User Which Using the Hashtags of 'groups of Death' - SEO Hero," accessed May 23, 2018, https:// seoheronews.com/vk-hashtags.

7 Anastasia Taylor-Lind, *Fighters and Mourners of the Ukrainian Revolution*, accessed May 28, 2018, https://www.ted.com/talks/ anastasia_taylor_lind_fighters_and_mourners_of_the_ ukrainian_revolution.

8 Jacques Rancière and Gabriel Rockhill, *The Politics of Aesthetics: The Distribution of the Sensible* (New York: Bloomsbury Academic, 2016), 8.

9 For more about the use of social media in the Taksim Square demonstrations, see Zeynep Tufekci, *Twitter and Tear Gas: The Power and Fragility of Networked Protest* (New Haven, CT: Yale University Press, 2018).

10 Christopher Le Dantec, "The Right Way to Make Cities Smart," *The Atlantic*, May 20, 2014, https://www.theatlantic.com/technology/archive/2014/05/the-right-way-to-make-cities-smart/370900/.

#Slogan

1 J. L. Austin, *How to Do Things with Words*, ed. James Opie Urmson, Marina Sbisa, and Alec Wilder (Cambridge: Harvard University Press, 1976), 94–108.

2 Judith Butler, *Notes toward a Performative Theory of Assembly* (Cambridge: Harvard University Press, 2018), 28–29.

3 Moya Bailey, "#transform(Ing)DH Writing and Research: An Autoethnography of Digital Humanities and Feminist Ethics" 9, no. 2 (2015), http://www.digitalhumanities.org/dhq/vol/9/2/000209/000209.html.

4 Zahara Hill, "Black Woman Tarana Burke Founded The 'Me Too' Movement," *Ebony*, October 18, 2017, http://www.ebony.com/news-views/black-woman-me-too-movement-tarana-burke-alyssa-milano#axzz565E7wJXC.

5 Mikki Kendall, "#SolidarityIsForWhiteWomen: Women of Color's Issue with Digital Feminism," *The Guardian*, August 14, 2013, https://www.theguardian.com/commentisfree/2013/aug/14/solidarityisforwhitewomen-hashtag-feminism.

#Brand

1 Ken Johnson, "Review: 'Ennion,' at the Met, Profiles an Ancient Glassmaker," *New York Times*, March 5, 2015, sec. Art &

Design, https://www.nytimes.com/2015/03/06/arts/design/review-ennion-at-the-met-profiles-an-ancient-glassmaker.html.

2 Alice E. Marwick, *Status Update - Celebrity, Publicity, and Branding in the Social Media Age* (New Haven: Yale University Press, 2015).

3 See Crystal Abidin, "Layers of Identity," *Real Life* (blog), April 16, 2018, http://reallifemag.com/layers-of-identity/ for more granular descriptions of these processes.

#Origin

1 Joan Donovan, "Technologies of Social Change: Mapping the Infrastructure of the Occupy Movement from #OccupyWallStreet to #OccupySandy" (UC San Diego, 2015), https://escholarship.org/uc/item/6vh0q283.

2 Alicia Garza, "A Herstory of the #BlackLivesMatter Movement by Alicia Garza," *The Feminist Wire* (blog), October 7, 2014, http://www.thefeministwire.com/2014/10/blacklivesmatter-2/.

#Noise

1 Hope Jahren, *Lab Girl* (New York: Vintage, 2017), 37.

2 Richard Horgan, "Hawaii Scientist Hijacks Seventeen Magazine Hashtag," accessed July 14, 2018, https://www.adweek.com/digital/seventeen-magazine-manicuremonday-hope-jahren/.

3   Michele White, "How 'Your Hands Look' and 'What They Can Do': #ManicureMonday, Twitter, and Useful Media," *Feminist Media Histories* 1, no. 2 (April 1, 2015): 4–36.

4   For more on this subject, see Michael Ohl and Elisabeth Lauffer (trans.), *The Art of Naming* (Cambridge: MIT Press, 2018).

#Chatter

1   John Steinbeck, *Cannery Row*, Centennial Edition (New York: Penguin Books, 2002), 21.

2   Suey Park and Eunsong Kim, "We Want To #CancelColbert," *Time*, March 28, 2014, http://time.com/42174/we-want-to-cancelcolbert/.

3   Eunsong Kim, "The Politics of Trending," *Model View Culture*, accessed April 13, 2018, https://modelviewculture.com/pieces/the-politics-of-trending.

4   Dorothy Kim and Eunsong Kim, "The #TwitterEthics Manifesto," *Model View Culture*, accessed April 13, 2018, https://modelviewculture.com/pieces/the-twitterethics-manifesto.

#File

1   Max Weber, *Max Weber on Capitalism, Bureaucracy and Religion*, ed. Stanislav Andreski (Abingdon, UK: Routledge, 2006).

2   David Weinberger, *Everything Is Miscellaneous: The Power of the New Digital Disorder* (New York: Henry Holt, 2008).

3 Hend S. Al-Khalifa and Hugh C. Davis, "Towards Better Understanding of Folksonomic Patterns," in *Proceedings of the Eighteenth Conference on Hypertext and Hypermedia*, HT '07 (New York: ACM, 2007), 163–66.

4 Sanford Berman, *Prejudices and Antipathies: A Tract on the LC Subject Heads Concerning People* (Jefferson, NC: McFarland, 2014).

5 Dorothy Berry, "*Umbra Search African American History*: Aggregating African American Digital Archives," *Parameters* (blog), accessed January 27, 2018, http://parameters.ssrc.or g/2016/12/umbra-search-african-american-history-aggrega ting-african-american-digital-archives.

6 Geoffrey C. Bowker and Susan Leigh Star, *Sorting Things Out: Classification and Its Consequences* (Cambridge: MIT Press, 1999).

7 Susan Leigh Star and James R. Griesemer, "Institutional Ecology, 'Translations' and Boundary Objects: Amateurs and Professionals in Berkeley's Museum of Vertebrate Zoology, 1907-39," *Social Studies of Science* 19, no. 3 (1989): 387–420.

8 Katherine Hayles, *How We Became Posthuman: Virtual Bodies in Cybernetics, Literature, and Informatics* (Chicago: University of Chicago Press, 1999).

#Metadata

1 Fred Ricthin, "Four Corners Metadata," NPPA, August 16, 2017, https://nppa.org/magazine/four-corners-metadata.

2 Michael E. Ruane, "A Grisly Photo of a Saigon Execution 50 Years Ago Shocked the World and Helped End the War,"

Washington Post, February 1, 2018, sec. Retropolis, https://www.washingtonpost.com/news/retropolis/wp/2018/02/01/a-grisly-photo-of-a-saigon-execution-50-years-ago-shocked-the-world-and-helped-end-the-war/.

3   Susan Sontag, *Regarding the Pain of Others* (New York: Picador, 2004), 59–60.

4   "See How a Single Photo from Vietnam Helped Fuel the Anti-War Movement," 100 Photographs | The Most Influential Images of All Time, accessed April 21, 2018, http://100photos.time.com/photos/eddie-adams-saigon-execution.

5   Marshall McLuhan, *Understanding Media: The Extensions of Man*, ed. Lewis H Lapham (Cambridge: MIT Press, 1994), 7.

INDEX

Abidin, Crystal 80–3, 111
Adams, Eddie 125–6
African American Policy
    Forum 36
Āghā-Soltān, Nedā 27
Al-Khalifa, Hend 115–16
Arab Spring 2, 23
ASCII coding 14–15
Asplund, Lauren 15
@DevGriffin618 95
@emily.e.dickey 76
@jennimiller 29 76
@mayishahaleema 25–6
@sassycrass 71
Austin, J. L. 63

Bailey, Moya 65–6
Banerjee, Aryana 29
Bano, Asifa 36
BarCamps 19
Baudot, Émile 14
Bell, Alexander Graham 10, 21
Benjamin, Walter 123
Berman, Sanford 116

Berry, Dorothy 117
Bhasin, Kamla 26
Blank Noise 25–6, 30–1, 32,
    35–6
Bowker, Geoffrey 118
Breakthrough 31–2, 33
Brown, Michael 26–7, 38,
    48, 51, 86, 95, 109, 117
Burke, Tarana 68–70
Butler, Judith 64–5

Callimachus 121
Cameron, David 62
Castells, Manuel 41
Charlie Hebdo attack 66
Cheng, Wendy 81–2
Chua, Jamie 82
Clinton, Hillary 43, 70–1
Colbert Report, The (TV
    show) 100, 103–4, 107
Cool, Jennifer 21–2, 24
Cornell, Joseph 123
Crenshaw, Kimberlé 36
Cullors, Patrisse 86

Dappy (Costadinos
    Contostavlos)   6
Davis, Hugh   115
Dorsey, Jack   21, 22
Durov, Nikolai   50
Durov, Pavel   50
Dvorovy, Maksym   46–7

Edison, Thomas   10
Eisenstein, Sergei   54
emojis   68, 76–7, 128
Ennion   78
Erdoğan, Recep Tayyip   56
Euripides   114

Facebook   48, 49, 67
Fedchenko, Yevhen   49
"foobar"   19–20
Four Corners (software
    platform)   125
Foursquare   41

Garza, Alicia   86–7
Google   20
Griesemer, James   120

Halappanavar, Savita   27
hash character (#)   2–3, 13,
    14–18
Hashtag bar (Kiev)   39–42
#BlackLivesMatter   67, 84,
    85, 86–7, 117
#CancelColbert   100–8

#Ferguson, *see* Brown,
    Michael
#ManicureMonday   94,
    96–8
#MeToo   67–70
#OccupyWallStreet   84, 85–6,
    87, 109
hashtags
    activist uses   3, 25–6,
        30–8, 42, 45–57, 109
    advertising and
        promotional uses   1, 3,
        57, 77, 79–80
    automatic   128–9
    brand names   4, 75–84
    commemorative uses   1,
        26–7, 58
    communal (solidarity/
        camaraderie) uses   47,
        49, 63, 65–7, 70–3
    defined   2
    duplicate uses   27, 29, 32
    earliest uses   19–24
    effective qualities   3–4,
        5, 26
    hijacking   4, 93–8
    miscellaneous uses   61–3
    monetizing   39–40
    mundane uses   23
    place names   38, 42–59,
        90–1
    political uses   1–2, 47, 71
    shortcut uses   57

slogan uses   61–74, 102
threatening uses   1, 50
victims' names   26–9,
  36–7, 51
visibility uses   65–6, 108
Hayles, Katherine   122
Heng, Peggy   80
Hester, Wendy
  America   123–4
How I Met Your Mother
  (TV show)   102–3
Houston, Keith   15

identity politics   71
Indian feminists   25–6, 30–4
India's Daughter
  (documentary)   34–5
influencers   80–3
Instagram   25–6, 41, 49, 50,
  54, 67, 75, 77
Internet Relay Chat   20–1
Internet Ruined My Life, The
  (TV show)   107

Jahren, Hope   93–7
Jaiku   20
Johnson, Jessica Marie
  119–20
Judd, Ashley   68

Kelty, Christopher   24
Kendall, Mikki   73–4
Kennedy, John F.   9

Kerr, Doug   14, 15
Kim, Dorothy   111
Kim, Eunsong   99, 100,
  105–12
Koleda, Maria   50
Kruk, Kateryna   45–6, 49,
  50, 53
Kutcher, Ashton   23

Le Dantec, Christopher   47
Leonsis, Ted   21
Linton, Louise   75–7
Loan, Nguyễn Ngọc   126
Lytvyn, Andrew   39

machine-to-machine
  communication   7–8,
  127–9
MacPherson, Don   17
Maidan Nezalezhnosti   42,
  43–6, 51, 54, 58–9
Martin, Trayvob   86
Marwick, Alice   80
Mattern, Shannon   121
McLuhan, Marshall   130
Messina, Chris   19–21, 23
metadata   2–3, 54, 63, 100,
  109–10, 112, 115–22,
  123–30
Milano, Alyssa   67
Mock, Janet   65
Moroz, Vitaliy   46–7
Morse, Samuel   14, 21

MySpace   68

Neshevets, Natalia   53
Northup, Solomon   120

Obama, Michelle   65
octothorpe   17
O'Reilly, Tim   19

Park, Suey   100, 101–8
Patheja, Jasmeen   25, 30–1,
      34, 111
Perry, Katy   71
public square concept   41,
      42–3, 55, 56, 58

racial issues   68, 72–4, 100–8,
      117–19
Radynski, Oleksiy   54–5
Rancière, Jacques   55, 57
Raphael   79
"recursive public"   24

Safire, William   17–18
Sagolla, Dom   22
Saigon Execution   125–7
Sakr, Laila Shereen   89–91,
      111
Schwyzer, Hugo   73–4
Sentsov, Oleg   51
Sha'arawi, Huda   90
Singh Pandey, Jyoti   26, 27–8,
      29–30, 35

Snyder, Dan   104
Software Studies Lab   41
Sontag, Susan   126
Sophilos   79
Spartacus (film)   66
speech acts   63–5
Star, Susan Leigh   118, 120–1
Steinbeck, John   101
Supreme Court rulings   42–3
Sushchenko, Roman   51
Swift, Taylor   68

Tahrir Square   43, 89–91
Takru, Radhika   31–2, 33
Taksim Square   56–7
Taylor, Crystal   21–3
Taylor-Lind, Anastasia   52–3
telegraph   7, 14, 21
telephones   3, 8, 9–18, 21
Teletype   2, 14–15
text messaging   22–3, 34
trending topics   3, 6, 27,
      47–8, 70, 72, 81, 102,
      108–9
trolling and
      cyberstalking   33,
      104–5, 107–8, 111
Trump, Donald   61, 62
Tufekci, Zeynep   48
Turkish feminists   1
Twitter   19–24, 32, 48, 49, 67,
      100, 108
typewriters   2, 15–16

Udwin, Leslee   34–5
Ukrainian uprising   41–2, 43,
      44–55, 58–9

Vertov, Dziga   54
"visual culture"   53
Visual Culture Research
      Center   53, 54
VK (VKontakte)   49–50

Wallace, Alexandra   101
Weber, Max   113
Wedgwood and Sons   79

Weinberger, David   115
Weinstein, Harvey   67, 69
White, Michele   96
Winfrey, Oprah   23

Yanukovych,
      Viktor   41, 45
Yousafzai, Malala   65
YouTube   54–5

Zenodotus   121
Zimmerman, George   86
Zuccotti Park   85–6